Learning Places: *Real Love*

This book is a serious attempt to share some of the simple yet profound principles that are involved in effectively loving God, loving self and loving one another. Love is a truly remarkable and mysterious phenomenon, which in large part has eluded human definition. It is a heavenly agent operating in the earthly domain. I have sought within these pages to share openly, honestly, frankly and fairly some of my key lifetime experiences and learning in this area. Love can bring great pain and sorrow, but also has the power to engender the most euphoric, mind blowing and life changing experiences which human-beings are able to hope for, cope with or even contain, in our current earthly form.

Love embodies the raw, deep, earthy, passionate and fundamentally basic human chemistry... as well as the most lofty, sophisticated, esoteric, indescribable and intangible aspects of the human spirit and emotions! And these can all be experienced at the very same time! In the same instant! A truly marvellous paradigm!

I trust you will find this true-life account helpful, uplifting and life changing.

By David Apelt

Other Publications by David Apelt:-

Learning Places: Beginnings   2012

Learning Places: Weeping Saints   2014

Learning Places: *Real Love*
ISBN: 978-0-646-95025-9

All Rights Reserved
Copyright © 2016 by Leon David Chris Apelt
No part of this publication may be reproduced, stored or transmitted in any form or by any means without the prior permission of the author.

The only exception is for brief quotations for printed reviews and should always be accompanied by appropriate reference.

Front Cover Art is used with permission and is a copy of the original - Doves Eyes - by Ilse Kleyn at www.artofKleyn.com

Distributed by The LDC & JO Apelt
Family Trust PO Box 2818 Rowville.
Vic. Australia. 3178
www.learningplaces.org.au

Acknowledgements

In writing this book I would like to thank: Mum who always told me I could do whatever I set my heart upon, and who always demonstrated her love and faithfulness through words of affirmation and in the way she gave herself tirelessly to her husband, her marriage, her children and the numerous family endeavours which we explored together; Dad, who being a man of few words, showed his love through his actions in seeking to care and provide for our family. My father demonstrated that if you live and work faithfully and responsibly in life you will achieve your dreams; June my beautiful, gifted, capable, intuitive, creative, loving, wonderful wife who shared 36 delightful and fulfilling years of marriage with me; My amazing clever and legendary children and grandchildren who have brought me such joy and taught me so much; and then there are all my many other influential friends, family, colleagues and acquaintances in life and work.

There are so many who have gone before and journeyed with me in this rich and eventful lifetime, as well as demonstrated that everyone matters, and we can each make a very real difference in this world.

Thank You, One and All.

Contents

Prologue

Chapter 1 - Awakening of Young Love   1

Chapter 2 - The One   11

Chapter 3 - Courting with Destiny   15

Chapter 4 - Genesis of Love   16

Chapter 5 - Delicate Dance of Love   20

Chapter 6 - The Engagement   25

Chapter 7 - Romance by Distance   32

Chapter 8 - The Wedding   39

Chapter 9 - Attraction and Healthy Relationships   49

Chapter 10 - Advanced Attraction and Intimacy   88

Chapter 11 - Agape Based Marriage and Family   96

Chapter 12 - Agape Based Church and Community   103

Chapter 13 - Agape with Enemies   121

Chapter 14 - Miracles and Mysteries of Agape   125

Chapter 15 – Conclusion   127

Prologue

My heart is literally burning within me with a sense of passion and urgency... to share something really important with you. I have discovered that there is this fascinating and mysterious form of Love, existing in the world today, called Agape, which Judeo-Christians emphasize. It is the heart and soul of the Gospel... the good news about the Coming of The Lord Jesus Christ and has made possible the *grand healing of hearts* and the *great reconciliation* of God and man... which is in progress right now as we speak.

This love is delicate, elusive, wonderful and ethereal in shape and form, yet when experienced it is so deeply and profoundly moving, amazing, fulfilling, delightful and life changing, that one will never again be satisfied with anything less. It is so sweet, fragrant, beautiful, peaceful, joyful, ecstatic, desirable and ultimately restorative... yet embodies such compelling power to bring radical change to the hearts and circumstances of men, women and children... and to make life, relationships, marriage, family and community so much more enjoyable and satisfying... as well as to ultimately impact the whole world for good.

It is so important however that this love remains in its *pure* form... and does not become twisted or diluted... for then it is no longer Agape.

This book seeks to reflect upon, describe, analyse and share true stories about this love, in contrast with other forms of love, like phileo (friendship and family love) and eros (sexually intimate love)... in a way which will help define its nature and essence. This will hopefully assist in creating a mental model of what agape is really like. First-hand accounts and observations also seek to demonstrate what it is, what it is not, and describe its effects & benefits.

The writer has shared many of his own innermost thoughts, feelings, emotions, reasoning and experiences... and those of his late wife, as well as other trusted male and female friends, in order to give a more complete picture and to help expose some of the mystery. This can be thought provoking, deeply moving and even troubling at times.

Please join me on this journey to discover how beautiful, compelling and attractive this Love really is, and observe the power that it has to bring healing & restoration, personally, corporately, regionally and nationally.

My first book 'Learning Places: Beginnings' is also themed on this Love.

Please enjoy!

David Apelt.

Chapter 1 - Awakening of Young Love

It was a cool, cloudy Sunday afternoon in 1970 and I had just enjoyed worship at the local Presbyterian Church, in the small thriving country town of Kingaroy in Queensland, Australia, nestled in a most Idyllic and beautiful farming area called the South Burnett. This town is noted for its red, volcanic soil which can grow almost anything, but will infiltrate and stain everything it comes in contact with. I painfully and vividly recall that having been stained, it was a massive effort to remove from clothes and shoes. This richly coloured soil even caused terrible staining to the skin, should someone be regularly exposed to the dastardly substance. In those days Kingaroy district was renowned for the successful farming of peanuts... and also navy beans which are used in the making of the world famous baked-beans, a celebrated and nutritious staple food of the day.

As an aside, the Kingaroy region was also the home of a well-known and very effective, bold, no nonsense, down to earth politician for whom I had a great deal of respect. He had traditional family and community values, a gift for getting to the heart of the matter and was a man of action. Once having decided what needed to be done, he had the courage of his convictions to stand by what he believed and would simply make things happen.

Soon after being transferred to this simple yet progressive and influential country town, I had experienced the end of an embryonic, mildly intoxicating relationship with a very beautiful, intelligent and intriguing young woman who had caught my attention in another small, country town where I used to live and work with the local bank. Initially, I was extremely saddened and disappointed by her apparent reluctance to respond to my desire to spend more time with her. However, her elusiveness and reasons for not being willing to progress our relationship ultimately made sense to me and I had to resolve to bring to a close any thoughts of us ever being together. This was initially very difficult, and I had to process a lot of sadness, because I had seriously begun to open up my heart and spirit to this possibility. I remember shedding many tears, which in the main were quiet and private... and this went on for weeks. Slowly however I began to come to a knowing that we were not meant to be together. This was very sad and very final, but I knew I had to face up to this reality, process the difficult feelings... resolve them in my heart and mind and proceed to move on.

There were also other times I recall, in earlier years, prior to this first potentially serious relationship, which helped me to learn various aspects of what it meant to be attracted to the opposite sex:-

For example, in year eight at the delicate young age of thirteen or so, I recall there was this cute, finely built, but appropriately curvaceous, medium height, delicate, thoughtful and seemingly shy, but quite sophisticated young lady, who came to our school for just one year. She had the finest golden, brown-blonde, curly, well-presented hair, which I had ever seen, and I marvelled that there never seemed to be a strand out of place. She carried herself beautifully and elegantly, erect and stylish as if she had been to a deportment or modelling school. She had also rightly caught the attention of many of us discerning young men. Yet there was a problem. She seemed to either lack the ability to connect emotionally with any of us or alternatively maybe she thought she was a cut above us simple, young, uncomplicated country lads. I remember feeling very sad about this. Because she was very pretty and seemed to be a really nice person underneath her more serious and aloof exterior.

There was another experience a year later in year nine which demonstrated the power and craziness of young love. There was a young lady who lived on a farm about seventeen kilometres out of town. Now these were very early days, it had only been a year or so since I had begun to really seriously notice all these delightful young ladies, many of whom had been around me all the way through school. So, as inexperienced young men we therefore lacked confidence and in those days our age was considered far too young to have serious relationships with young ladies. Nevertheless, there she was in one of our classes. This stand-out little beauty, with long blonde hair, beautiful generous curves in all the right places and a delightful outgoing warm and contagiously friendly personality. She had this masterful ability to make all of the boys believe that we were special to her even though we rarely ever spent time talking with her. Well, there we were! What could we do? What should we do? Finally, after much thoughtful consideration, my two mates and I hatched this extravagant plan. We would ride our bikes out to her farm one Saturday morning, in the hope of getting just one small glimpse of her in her home environment. What an adventure. It took weeks to plan. These were the days when bicycles, at least the ones that we could afford to own, were not very durable, comfortable, long wearing or easy riding. During that journey all of our bikes had mechanical troubles. We almost turned back many times. But the prize of just one glimpse of this captivating young lady urged us on. By the time we got there though, we were walking, pushing our bikes, bruised and weary. It was getting late in the day, supplies were running low, and we were about five hundred meters from her house! But we got cold feet. We had not really considered what we might do if or when we actually got there. We did not know her parents. They were not expecting us, etc. So, we cut our losses, celebrated the fact that we had actually made the distance and turned our eyes toward home! With mixed and unfulfilled emotions in our hearts, we chatted contentedly and light- heartedly about our adventure and the journey home felt much shorter than the way out. We learned from this experience that the motivational power of young love can be very compelling.

Some years later, another even more memorable occasion occurred. There was this very pretty, intelligent, high spirited, mischievous and fun-loving young lady also living in the town in which I studied and worked prior to going to Kingaroy, who seemed like she might be mildly interested in me.

We used to have a great deal of light- hearted fun over the few years that I knew her, sparring and enjoying one another's attention and conversation. Well, it just so happened that one dark and elegantly moonlit night, with the most beautiful clear skies, and a myriad of diamond-like stars twinkling vigorously overhead... I vividly recall that I was given the privilege of driving her home in my beloved 1964 sleek pearl-white EH Holden Special Sedan, suitably lowered, with chrome fatties and red pinstripes! I remember this was a particularly unusual bonus occurrence because she usually had her own transport. After arriving at her home, and seemingly preparing to say goodbye and leave, she took me by surprise! Without saying a word, she made a quiet but very elegant, beautiful, well-executed and determined move on me. She rose up on her knees on the front seat and leaned across alluringly and delicately and gave me the most amazing, tender, loving and delightful kiss! @#?> Woh!... I wasn't expecting that! But of course, I didn't resist one iota and entered fully into the joy of the moment! Returning all the love and affection she had so generously lavished on me. It was a wonderful experience and mind-blowing! Now, I was a relatively young man, inexperienced in all these matters and the buzz of endorphins and hormones and such... were really explosive! This was in fact my very first kiss! And what a beautiful kiss it was! I was overcome. I didn't know what to say or do! But after savouring the moment for a short while, with deep feelings of affection and connection hanging there delicately in the air like an explosion of golden snowflakes... I think we finally gave each other knowing smiles and a long and abiding hug... then said our winsome good-nights and went our separate ways. I reflected on that special moment at length over the next few weeks and the beauty, wonder, affection, intimacy and closeness of that occasion. But sadly, I did not get a sense that we were meant to be together. So, I didn't follow through by making her a more serious offer. Although it was so very tempting at the time! What a delightful memory this is, even now, as I reminisce on this my journey of life and of love.

There were a few other really lovely young ladies in that town which had also caught my attention. Some I had even spent some very special times with, but they just didn't seem or feel as if they were meant to be... *The One...*

Now back to Kingaroy. Some six months later, after finding some semblance of peace in my life again, I was ripe, ready and fully prepared to find that ideal, young woman, to marry, settle down and start a family and future together. I had enjoyed my own family life very much and felt naturally drawn to the concept of marriage and the bounteous wonders of all that it entailed. Here I was standing outside that little Presbyterian Church, the membership of which had become seriously depleted and was generally aging and losing momentum. I happened to be talking casually with a young man whom I had only recently got to know and who eventually would become a lifelong friend, and key part of my extended family. He had been there much longer than I. I remember saying something like "Hey, Mate! Are there any other churches in this town, which might just have some desirable and eligible young ladies in attendance who could perhaps be suitable marriage partners for the likes of us worthy young fellows?" He mused, smiled cheekily, reflected thoughtfully for a moment and then began to speak...

Before going on, let's summarize and reflect for a moment on my various learning, from these and many other very real, life-impacting experiences, particularly regarding the nature and characteristics of Love. It occurs to me for example that:-

- Everyone on this earth, whether male or female, is basically and uniquely gifted, talented, capable, wonderful, beautiful, desirable and of great worth in a myriad of different ways
- We each have a foundational instinct within us which gives a deep yearning to both love and be loved
- A primary aspect of this love is to persistently seek out a connection with the Divine. This can be to varying degrees from subliminal to overtly conscious
- There is also an inherent desire and strong drive within human beings to seek out a serious and enduring bond of love between a man and a woman. This is naturally required to produce children and to socialize, extend and protect the human race. It seems to be a natural part of our psyche
- Any male and female couple has the potential to experience this bond with each other but there does seem to be some predisposition to the types of people to whom we are naturally drawn
- There also appears to be, if we are inclined to seek them out, a particular partner or soul mate that we are ideally suited to and meant to be with in life
- Finding a good match for your life partner can be the most wonderful, delightful, fulfilling and satisfying experience that a man and a woman can have in this life. It is worth the effort to be sure,

and I should add that all three forms of natural and supernatural love (described later) are designed to work effectively within and enrich this type of relationship
- In order to succeed in love, both the man and the woman need to have a strong desire for each other and the commitment to make it work
- It seems to me wasted effort to hold out for a serious love relationship to be reciprocated by someone who expresses no desire to do so
- We should always act in loving and respectful ways towards each other, but one cannot force someone to love them
- It is good however to make your intentions known when you have feelings for someone. Don't always wait to be asked or expect them to read your mind. But one must always be prepared for the possibility of a negative answer. Negative answers should always be gracious, loving, thoughtful and respectful. Ungracious or ruthless rejection in love has potential to seriously damage the human psyche, requiring various degrees of spiritual healing
- We should never lead someone to believe that there could be hope of a serious relationship if indeed you feel there is none. This is taking undue, unkind and unfair advantage
- Parents should give wise advice but not have undue influence to the point of forcing their son or daughter to marry or not marry someone. The final choice should always rest with the two potential lovers
- The various acts of serious intimate and ecstatic contact and intercourse between a man and a woman really do make a tangible connection

between them... body, soul and spirit. So, it is not wise to confuse ourselves or our partners with unduly intimate connection when we are not considering an enduring relationship
- Serious intimate contact and connection between lovers is designed to be ecstatic and explosively delightful, to the very depths and dizzy heights of our being. This is in order to seal and continually strengthen and reinforce the loving bond between the man and the women in an enduring relationship. Self-control and moderation is advised however, because the sheer ecstasy of these acts of pleasure, love and intimacy have the potential to become extremely addictive, obsessive or compulsive for one or both partners. If this is left unchecked there can also be a risk of unfaithfulness to a life partner, which invariably only brings devastating heart ache to all concerned
- Finally, some people will choose to be single or have singleness thrust upon them through life circumstances. This too is an honourable state to live in. Two forms of the three major types of love (agape and phileo) are open to, encouraged and work really well, providing wonderful fulfillment, for singles. The other form of love (eros) however is highly undesirable and not recommended because of the implied reasons above. I would say however I believe that if you really have a deep desire in your heart to marry and have a family, you should save yourself for that day. Hold onto that dream, in a balanced and wise fashion, without becoming obsessed and in most cases you will one day find the partner that you yearn for deeply, or alternatively they will find you.

Perhaps I've run ahead of myself a little here... However, these discoveries are all very foundational and critically important life- learning which came to me during my experiences of the awakening, emerging, developing, maturing and blossoming of love. Many of these topics are visited further in later chapters.

Chapter 2 - The One

So there I was in Kingaroy, with the question about the possibility of other suitable young ladies being available in this here town, still hanging precariously in the air. Then my mate said "Well actually, I think there is! I've heard that another church in the town is experiencing a mini revival and I believe they have a large group of young people who meet there!". "Aha! I said we must visit there then!"... and so we did without further delay! The very next week! On youth group night!

This was a small Church of Christ, way out on the edge of town, being led by a passionate and driven young pastor who was determined to see his generation encounter Jesus personally in his time. His fervour was legend. Being high spirited and opinionated he was extremely confident, though not always right, and later on I had the dubious 'joy' of becoming his favourite new target, for many of his dissertations on the various nuances of his pet topics. What a high price to pay in order to pursue young love! But I have to say, it was ultimately worth the 'pain' and 'suffering', in order to win the prize!

So there we were. We had arranged to meet at the church. I was feeling a little nervous. I was not overly confident in those days in interacting with young ladies and dealing with matters of the heart. Tentatively we marshalled up the necessary courage and walked into the room and found a place to sit discreetly at the back of the meeting. I don't remember all the details of that night, but I do remember walking into a veritable feast of attractive young ladies, the largest group I had seen in one place, at a church related gathering, in my whole life!

Initially, we just tried to relax and soak in the atmosphere. Checking out the lay of the land you might say. I was already very serious in my faith and respectful toward God and church, realizing the importance of these issues in daily life. Therefore, on the one hand being really respectful, reflective and meditative toward God, I could not help but notice the variety and natural beauty of spirit and body in this amazing group of young ladies. They were chatting animatedly, mingling and gathering informally in small groups before the meeting started.

Now as you can imagine, since I didn't know anyone, apart from my friend who had come with me, I remained at a distance initially and periodically my eyes would wander from one to the next thoughtfully processing first impressions of their personalities and the natural aspects of their beauty. I have this gift of being able to 'see' and 'feel' the spirit of people, to varying degrees, along with the normal, natural and healthy ability to sense and notice the various forms of beauty in a person of the opposite sex. Some were tall, some short, others medium height and all the sizes in between. Although enjoying the company and natural beauty of all women, for some unknown reason, I have always felt I would marry someone shorter than me. Then there was the variety of hair colours; naturally golden, blonde, brown, black and all manner of artificial alternatives. I realized later that although blondes would often catch my attention first, it was the brunettes whom I felt more comfortable with, for a strategic long-term relationship. Hair arrangements

Learning Places: *Real Love*

were short, long, curly, straight, fixed up, let down, ribbons, head bands, discreet black hairpins and all forms of bold colours! And the outfits! What a vista! Long dresses, medium and short miniskirts. Although they were frowned upon by the more religious of the day! Low cut, high cut, off the shoulder, on the shoulder. Showing little, showing lots! There were extroverts, introverts and all the flavours in between. It was obvious and to their credit, that every one of these pretty young ladies had gone to great lengths, to present themselves in the best possible light, on this very special gathering of the young people of the town. So the whole experience was exceedingly delightful, as you can imagine, but also very confusing, due to the smorgasbord of combinations, and as it were... possibilities!

After the group settled down, there were prayers, welcome, introductions and comments on the evening program. Then the praise and worship began. Suddenly something special happened. It wasn't just the presence of God in the meeting, although that was very evident, as best I could discern it in those days! What was really going on was my attention was being inextricably drawn to the beautiful young brunette, with shoulder length black hair, quietly yet confidently playing the piano in the most adorable way. There was something about her! I saw something, sensed something, heard something, and felt something, all in the same instant of time. Fascinating! She was truly stunning. Her jet-black hair was glistening and curling in all the right places and delicately augmented her satin smooth, olive skin. She carried herself well as she sat at the piano and her delicate hands moved deftly across the keyboard bringing forth the most delightful music. Her outfit was simple and well-presented and hugged her closely in all the right places. Something 'clicked' in my spirit. This could be the one. She certainly stood out from the crowd that night and had the most impact upon me out of all those truly pretty, engaging and delightful young ladies. Something had certainly happened in my spirit there that night!

Being a man of action, after the meeting had finished and a suitably discreet amount of time had passed. No more than five minutes I might add. I made a point of going over to see her at the piano and briefly said hello and introduced myself. It was then that I noticed she had the most warm, bright, sparkling, penetrating, friendly, inviting and engaging eyes. A disarming smile that immediately melted my heart, the cutest little pixie nose, fine features and a delicate, youthful, very feminine beauty and innocence which took my breath away! I had trouble carrying conversation with her because I was being so deeply moved at the time. She was obviously very shy and would have been just 18 years old. Yes, this one was very special and worthy of serious effort to get to know her better. Just as an aside I noticed that night, the 'music' book she was playing from did not have any music. Just the words and an indication of the key the song was in. She had a most wonderful gift with music, to experience it spiritually and play it by ear from her heart. That was the very beginning, the genesis of love, with my beautiful wife to be. Embryonic admittedly, but I was greatly impacted that night and immediately set about to see what this passionate, enthusiastic young country boy could do, in order to get to know her better, and perhaps win her heart!

Chapter 3 - Courting with Destiny

From a very young age, I sensed the importance of marriage and family, and always felt that this was to be part of my destiny. I was also certain that it was a very important, foundational building block for our society and way of life. Now, because of my experiences in early days of discovering and exploring young love, I was determined to consult with God this time, to ensure that this union was meant to be, and not going to be a false start, before I began to invest my life in seeking to pursue this beautiful young maiden. She was a delight to behold and brought joy to my soul, even from a distance, a real pleasure to be with and I had difficulty trying to stop thinking about her... But I needed to be sure!

So, I tried every prayer I knew. "Lord please takeaway my desire if she is not to be the one", "Cause her to lose interest in the possibility", "Take away my peace when I think about a future with her", "Put other roadblocks in our way"... "Don't let it happen if it's not of You", "Show me a sign Lord, for or against", "Reveal all the possible downsides to a relationship with her Lord", "As I begin to work toward the possibility, please show me what is right to do", and finally, "If I don't hear or feel any good reason to the contrary, by such and such a date, I will begin to seriously pursue this young lady, and leave the results up to You Lord!"

Chapter 4 - Genesis of Love

So the time had come. Destiny and romance filled the air with an eerie sense of sweet, simmering suspense. I was alert, energized and passionate, bristling with excitement and attuned and inspired by the possibility of encountering *Real Love*. I sensed the stakes were high and there was indeed an element of risk. But I was as ready as one could be, albeit a little insecure, tense and nervous about the possibility of things not working out again. But I was determined to make a move. She was worth fighting for.

Over a period of weeks, we had diligently attended this dynamic new youth group and entered into the fullness of all their programs and the delights of friendship and fellowship with its members. It was a fascinating exercise in experimenting with and developing our social skills, especially with the pretty young ladies.

Although there were other really interesting possible partners and some who even periodically made an allusion to interest in a relationship, try as I might, I could not take my mind, or my eyes, off that delightful little brunette. We had only experienced some quite brief encounters and simple conversations.

I visited her home a few times and met her family. She was one of six children living in very modest circumstances. She even got to ride in my dearly beloved EH Holden on a couple of brief occasions. The more I saw of her breathtaking, innocent and natural beauty, her quiet, fun-loving, thankful and respectful attitude, and the enjoyment, sincere delight and fulfillment she got out of the simple things of life, the more I felt drawn to her! Her only big dreams at that time in life were to get married to a nice young man who treated her well, have babies and go to the 'big city' to live one day. These were realistic and practical dreams, the makings of the very fabric of our Australian way of life, and totally consistent with my dreams, as well. My feelings toward her grew each day and a settled peace that I should make my feelings known.

I was keen to spend as much time with her as possible, without scaring her off. Time was short and precious. Working for a bank in those days meant at any time one could turn up at work and be directed to move within two weeks to another town on the other side of the state. So, one morning I plucked up courage to go into her place of work, in the early hours of the day, before the customers started to come, hoping to get an opportunity to make light conversation with her and to see if she was interested in having the beginnings of a relationship with me.

After greeting her gently but with unveiled enthusiasm, I very nervously sought for words to express my keen interest. "Sissy," I said, for she didn't really like her own name, June, and I had already selected a pet-name which I thought suited her. "Would you like to be my girlfriend?" I said tentatively with measured anxiety and hopeful enthusiasm. She had been sweeping the floor at the time and she purposefully put aside the broom and looked intently into my eyes, for what seemed like an eternity. Oops! I thought, maybe this wasn't going to turn out as I had dared to hope. I could see her beautiful mind processing the enormity of my question and her sweet gentle heart was searching, yearning, reaching out, pounding heavily, at the thought of adventure, romance and happiness, which she had always dreamed of and longed for. There surely was destiny in the heart of this young maiden. Yet her spirit was grappling with whether there was Divine purpose in a lifetime alliance with this particular young man, for she had already given her heart and personal commitment to follow and serve the Lord Jesus all the days of her life. What He had to say on this subject really mattered to her and she was hopeful, but not yet certain.

This was surely a vexing question for one so young. She would have still been just eighteen years old at the time. This moment could be the most wonderful beginning of the fulfillment of so many of her life dreams! Or indeed just more pain and confusion! Since, for one so young she had already been through a brief friendship with another young man that did not end well. Pain and disappointment were evident when she spoke of it.

So, here we were on the edge of the future, suspended in the enormity of the moment and me starting to doubt whether I had done the right thing and whether I had been premature in doing so. Then suddenly, heavenly genius! Something popped into my mind, and I said tentatively and probably quite clumsily, hoping to reduce the gravity of the situation, and before she had even uttered one word in response. "Sissy, I don't want you to sign your life away, I just want us to spend more quality time together, getting to know each other better, to see if there is any hope of us getting together in the future! What do you say?" To my delight she immediately said "Yes! I'd like that!" and gave me one of her most beautiful little fun loving cheeky and knowing smiles; a delicate yet firm little hug and we parted ways that day with a new spark in our spirit, and a skip in our step.

Chapter 5 - Delicate Dance of Love

Things changed forever that day in both of our hearts. A heightened new sense of excitement, anticipation, adventure and purpose began to emerge in our relationship. There was an increased desire to be together as much as we could. We would talk for hours, of dreams and hopes and plans, and who we really were in the private places of our hearts and minds. The spark of romance began to ignite as we thoughtfully, gently, hesitantly and delicately began to open up our hearts and spirits to each other, regarding the possibility of a serious future together as husband and wife. Marriage was a given for us in that we both understood the importance that this committed relationship has in providing stability and nurturing for children and extended families, and the foundational, positive and beneficial effect which it has on society. We had lived long enough to know that children longed for the love affection and affirmation of both their Mum and their Dad, and that this gave them balance and confidence in life. Having children was something we both hoped and dreamed would happen for us. Although we seriously acknowledged that conception is itself also a Divine miracle, an act of God, over which we have little or no control, and about which we cannot make assumptions or presumptions. We are totally at His mercy and favour. But we both dreamed of children, nevertheless. I think if we are meant to have children there is often a knowing which occurs in potential mothers and fathers, who will one day have children.

Life was busy though. We had full-time jobs and significant commitments with the church youth group and family and friends. We still managed to spend lots of time together. I would pick Junie up and take her to work in the legendary EH and visited her most days after work unless we had a commitment to go out, in which case I usually got to see her any way. The more I saw, experienced and learned of this delightful young lady, the more I began to desire her and began to seriously open up my heart to her and long for the day that we would be together.

It wasn't always clear sailing though because Junie's mum thought, and actually said on one or two occasions, that I was a cheeky, young upstart. This was probably right from her perspective at least. I certainly was not as experienced in the finer points of inter-personal and romantic relationships as one becomes later in life. I also felt the pressure in that I would almost certainly be transferred away from Kingaroy in the not-too-distant future as was the way of the banks in those days. There was even a time where Junie called our relationship off for a few days. This was seriously difficult for me and very unsettling, in that she had already captured a really big part of my heart and dreams. I said "Lord, is this the end?" and asked that if we are meant to be together would He please help us to get through this time. I was in agony and suspense, but I kept my concerns to myself... hoping beyond hope that all would be well. After a week of torture and a little cajoling and talking, sharing and negotiation she relented, and we picked up where we had left off and the romance moved a lot more quickly and seriously than before.

Her uncertainty at the time was understandable. Her family was very close and mine were much more insular and separate, mainly because life just seemed to take us all off to the four corners of Australia. I was quite confident for a relatively young man of just over 20 years and although she was an amazingly gifted, capable, delightful and beautiful woman, she did not have strong confidence in herself or her own abilities. She felt quite vulnerable in a serious relationship with a boyfriend who is over six feet tall, while she was just five feet, and he was at the beck and call of a large bank, who could transfer him anywhere in Queensland on the whim of some faceless head office personnel. Very much like being in the Army... And we had only been going steady now for a few short months. She was feeling the pressure of possibilities and was not sure whether she was ready. This was understandably really scary for this wonderful, gentle, delightful, young, country princess. Fortunately for me though, and for us, she had already begun to love me in deeper more mysterious and engaging ways and was committing more of herself to our relationship than she had ever experienced before. We were both starting to experience that weird, wonderful, captivating and intoxicating delight called falling in love!

Sadly however, it was just a few short months later I turned up at work on December 16th, 1970, and there in dispatches was a short one-page memo which advised me that I had been appointed to Queensland relieving staff and directed me to report to Pialba branch in Hervey Bay. Argghh! Darn! This hit me like a full-on jumping kick to the chest with both feet! I knew it would inevitably come but it was still a shock. This meant I would be transferred at short notice, on short assignments of just a few weeks, all over Queensland to relieve bank officers who were on leave. This first assignment was just over three hours' drive away from Kingaroy, but there are towns in Queensland which are two days drive away. I didn't want to tell Junie, but I had to, and sooner rather than later! As usual they had only given me two weeks' notice. I can still feel the intense emotion of this occasion as I write these words. This meant our budding romance would have to operate by long distance.

When I told Junie, she cried. This broke my heart too and I could barely hold back the tears. I was crying inside my heart. This is a really weird experience but is something I've had to live with my whole life. My tear ducts don't seem to be able to release enough fluid to have a really good cry. Another thing I didn't like was seeing my beautiful, new girlfriend in tears. Particularly when I knew there was nothing I could do to change the circumstances. We had known this would happen, but the practicalities don't hit until you have a real-life scenario. Those two weeks went like wild-fire and soon it was time to leave. It was heartbreaking. But we had laid a plan. If I was within driving distance, up to say three and a half hours, I would try to come home once a month. Otherwise, we'd have to take it case by case. I boarded with a lovely family in Kingaroy who were really good friends and they welcomed me home whenever I could make it. But sadly, it was not very often. In the meantime, we surmised that our love would continue to grow and we would try to manage the yearning by writing letters to each other and posting at least one per week. This worked really well and was the best that technology could provide cost effectively in those days. Those letters were very therapeutic in that we had to try to capture our feelings and longings in words that would encourage and console and strengthen our love. I think that was part of the journey for me in learning the skills of writing. Many of those letters were really deeply moving and helped us get through the long weeks and months of separation. I don't think any of those letters still exist today. I was just thinking I'd really love to read them again. These types of mementos become really precious once your life partner has died. They were full of love and longing, yearning, warmth and tenderness, of hope, increasing anticipation and a growing desire for intimacy, as we valiantly sought to express, what was happening in our heart, and in our lives over that interminable distance. Just when we thought we could bear it no more it was time to visit. But the weekends were too short, and long weekends were so few. Our meetings became more intense and partings more painful.

Chapter 6 - The Engagement

Now as you can imagine, I really felt a sense of urgency and began to turn my mind and my heart more seriously toward the possibility and timing of getting engaged. The process of negotiating our relationship and working towards our engagement had to be worked out over long periods of separation, which I will refer to further in the next chapter. Things which would have been simple while we were both in the same town became quite challenging and more complex by long distance. However, love seemed to find a way and we managed somehow.

Getting engaged was a big step, which I know Junie looked forward to. But it was a really important milestone, and I didn't want her to feel unduly pressured. I am a gifted risk manager, and I did everything possible to make sure that I knew she would say yes before I proposed. I also secretly selected two really special dates that seemed to me to be destiny dates for us. The 17th of July 1971 and the 27th of May 1972. Both Saturdays, which was the ideal day for us to get married, and they were approximately a year apart, which was a good length for an engagement. They were both miraculously reversible. 17/7/71 and 27/5/72. And there was also a triple seven in the middle of our engagement date, which is a heavenly sign of perfection. So, I centred my campaign upon these particular and target-worthy dates.

We had already selected the type of ring which she would like if we ever got engaged. I'm just looking at it now and remembering how tiny her beautiful, elegant little fingers were. The ring barely fits on the first knuckle of my smallest finger. It is a simple gold band with an elevated eight-sided inverted golden cone which holds the larger centre diamond in place, and two parallel tiny gold pillars on both sides each held in place by a triangle of gold filled with tiny diamonds. It is a truly lovely ring.

Even now, as I hold this tiny ring respectfully in my hand, I am reminded of the Divine experience of Love, which we had the joy to share in this world for a wonderful thirty-six years of marriage. The memories flood into my spirit, of hard times, good times, and excellent times, as well as times where we had to just grin and bear it and walk in faith through the valleys of the shadows of death, until release came. What a lovely memento of our life together. Her wedding ring I did not keep, it was on her finger as a sign of my eternal love for her, when she was interred in the beautiful Lilydale Garden Cemetery, facing the sunrise each day. It was at sunrise too, when she turned her head towards the light and went to meet the Lord Jesus, on the golden morning of 6th of September 2008. Those were painful days as I processed the loss of the one I loved with all my heart. The One with whom I had become one together. I miss her so. Even now these seven years later.

Well, it took me a few months after I left Kingaroy to negotiate and arrange all that was necessary and to be confident enough in our relationship to be ready to propose. So, there we were on my extended holiday break over Easter in 1971. It was a beautiful, moonlight night in Kingaroy and we had just been out on a date and spent some really wonderful time together. We were sitting talking animatedly and intimately, in the front seat of my pride and joy. Cars in those days usually had bench seats instead of bucket seats, so couples could get much closer together without all the paraphernalia in between. I positioned myself with intent and looked deeply into the eyes of this amazing and breathtakingly beautiful young woman, whom I now loved more than any other person on the face of the earth, and who I was beginning to love in a way I had never loved a woman before. She was my very first really serious girlfriend, so I had never experienced the intensity of these feelings before in my whole life. It all felt very ethereal. The emotions were unique, strange, powerful, breathtaking, exciting, enlivening, deeply moving and arousing in the deepest part of my being.

My heart was pounding with anticipation and excitement. This was a once in a lifetime experience. No room for error. But I was as confident as any young man can be. And I was prepared to give her my heart... along with all my love... and honour my word to love her, respect, protect, provide and be at her side all the days of her life. I knew the deal and I was always a man of my word. The weight of this moment was not lost on me.

So I took a deep breath, cleared my throat nervously and said softly, but with great intent, "Miss Junie Olive Rogerson" (pregnant pause for maximum effect) "Will you please marry me?" There... I finally did it! I thought to myself! I'd been building up to this moment for months. This was it! The Ultimate Proposal! A once in a lifetime event! The impact of what I had just done was starting to sink into my spirit. Today I had stepped out onto the water! I'd put my heart on the line!

Risked everything for a most wonderful woman, whom I was beginning to love more deeply every day! I had now made a proposal, which if agreed to, would affect me personally and profoundly for the remainder of my natural life, and this would be the beginning of a new marriage, a new family and another dynasty, with potentially amazing destiny. Two clans which had never had anything to do with each other would potentially be aligned and connected together through this sacred act of marriage. However, what would she say, how many lifetimes would I have to wait to get her answer. Was she ready? A few months ago, there had been doubts, some family issues to be resolved, and hot and heavy negotiations. I had asked her Mum and Dad in principle. They had both said yes, but with some provisos. So here I was hanging in mid-air, seeing my life flash before me and thinking a thousand thoughts a minute...

Then finally, after what seemed an eternity, this beautiful young maiden, who had ignited something unique, intimate and powerful within my spirit, opened her cute little mouth. I saw her lips move. My heart skipped a beat and then I heard her sweet voice say, quietly but confidently, "Yes I will, Mr. Davie Apelt." There was an adventuresome sparkle in her eyes, which were beginning to glisten with happy tears, and the hint of a cheeky but loving smile crept gently across her beautiful angelic face.

Then she surprised me totally. This beautiful woman, who had just committed to share her whole life with me, lent across, took a hold of my face gently in both hands and gave me the most wonderful delicate but intimate and delightful kiss upon my lips. This was something she had never done before. She had made a decision not to kiss her man until or unless they were engaged. This was her first kiss! This was our first kiss! And was a very significant and sacrificial act of love, one that would have cost her a great deal emotionally. She was risking an act of love that she had never tried or experienced before... and it was beautiful. Now, you might be tempted to compare kisses at this point. But I didn't, It did not even enter my mind, I was so delighted that she had accepted my proposal, and that satin soft, cool yet delightfully warm, caress of a kiss, from the woman I was about to marry, meant the world to me. And during the 36 years which we were destined to have together on this earth, she demonstrated her love in such a myriad of different ways, which totally satisfied our passion for each other, and powerfully and practically demonstrated her love, commitment and faithfulness to me, our marriage and our family. She had an enormous capacity for love and compassion which grew stronger over the years and caused her to be loved and appreciated by everyone she met. Even in death, the very memory of her, still influences so many thousands of people all over the earth and helps to make the world a better place. She was an adorable and delightful woman whom I enjoyed immensely and deeply, every moment that we spent together.

I learned during those days that June's rules about what was and wasn't appropriate while we were boy and girlfriend, made perfectly good sense. For example, if we had been kissing, every time we met, in the way that I had experienced for my first kiss, then I seriously doubt we would have been able to refrain from actually making love. This would have meant that we had nothing to look forward to when we were married. It probably would also have caused things to be very awkward between us, and would have been a very serious problem indeed, if we had ultimately chosen not to marry.

Yes, it was a real blessing that we were both virgins when we married. It meant that we were both on an even footing when exploring together the novel and wonderful intimacies and delights of making love. It also meant that there were no awkward moments to experience, when probing questions were asked, which my precious wife Junie often loved to do! There were no comparisons able to be made, consciously or subconsciously, and there was no need for embarrassing secrets to be kept from one another. It is certainly the ideal and highly recommended. The alternative can potentially create highly complex situations and emotions and can even cause deep heart-ache for either or both parties. Issues of low self-esteem, jealousy, control or even a basic underlying lack of trust can develop or be exacerbated. If either party has had earlier sexual experience, it is important that this is shared before entering into a relationship, so that the emotions, implications and practicalities can ideally be discussed, processed, forgiven and hopefully resolved. Don't be disheartened though, if you have had prior sexual liaisons. Most issues can potentially be resolved, both practically and spiritually, through the selfless love and goodwill of both partners. However, as you can see, it just makes life and a new relationship, an order of magnitude more difficult to build on a strong and sure foundation.

I also reflected at this point that by today's standards we were seriously considering entering into marriage at a relatively young and tender age. When we were married, I was just 22 and June was almost 20 years of age. With hindsight I can also see that this is potentially good as well. It meant that instead of being fully matured and set in our ways individually, we could explore the journey of life, growth, development and maturity together as a couple and potentially as a family. This too has some serious benefits as long as it is done well. Each partner for example needs space to explore their individuality as well as being part of a couple. The gifts, talents and capabilities of the two individuals can then effectively and maturely complement each other and they become a marriage of committed equals. Rather than for example one totally or unfairly subsumed by the other, or alternatively both of them disappearing into a state of coupleness with no individual identities.

Well, then the really hard work commenced. Wedding plans and negotiations and madly trying to save as much money as we could to setup and support our new married life together. Neither of us had very much in the way of savings. Then there was the endless stress of driving long distances; in-frequent times together; and the uncertainty of never being sure when I would be directed by my employer to move on to another town.

Chapter 7 - Romance by Distance

For seventeen months we had to endure the challenges of a long- distance relationship with irregular and unpredictable times of encounter. There were so many very practical issues which created undue pressure on the developing intricacies of young love. For example, phone calls in those days were inordinately expensive, as was fuel for the car... and we needed to save money. So, this was a really strong tension, and mobile phones and internet where not available. Therefore, having no technology, expensive telephone calls, long distances and costly travel, all took their toll on our relationship. It took virtually one whole day just to drive there and back, so this would only leave us one full day together on a normal weekend. This was so depressing for new lovers growing deeper in love day by day and experiencing an increased yearning to spend more time together.

During these times, I learned that absence does make the heart grow fonder for the one you love and are missing so very much. I also learned that it is not a good thing to drive late into the night after a long day of working or socializing. I have since chosen not to do it unless absolutely necessary. I prefer now to get a good night's sleep and rise early between one am and three am, then drive on into the morning of the new day. This is much less risky and means one can travel very long distances and still allow safe arrival at your destination before the sun begins to set. There were so many times I recall when angels literally intervened directly in my circumstances to save my life and get me home to see my Beloved, or back to work after seeing her. It was with great reluctance, a heavy heart and teary eyes that I would leave her each time and have to face those gruelling journeys back to work the next day.

Here are a few accounts of Divine intervention. One rainy night heading home from Kingaroy to Bundaberg, where I had only just recently been posted on an assignment for some weeks, I had already been traveling for some time, through teeming rain, when the weather started to clear and it suddenly stopped raining, for which I was greatly appreciative. I was moving quickly on a clear road within the speed limit of course, when I entered a long sweeping bend in the road curving gently to the left then leveling out. All of sudden I realized I was fast approaching a two lane, unlit bridge. It was very dark with no stars or moonlight. As I got closer, I realized with a sudden shock, there seemed to be water on the road. So I began to slow down. Then Suddenly I realized this was deep water, and braking heavily, I managed to stop only a few meters from the edge. When I quickly surveyed the situation, my heart sank. This water was at least two meters deep and running fast! Had I not been able to stop in time I would have been dead for sure. Swept away in those terrible flood waters! This was a massive river, and it must have been a flash flood because there were no road signs or blockades, and no emergency services people had yet arrived. You can imagine how I felt. I was relieving a senior teller-general clerk at this branch, and I had combinations to the strong room and safes and various keys to this and that. It would totally disrupt the branch if I didn't turn up. I would also have felt very remorseful too, since I had really struggled as to whether I should do the run home to Kingaroy from that town or hold out for a future possibility. But my love for Junie was growing stronger by the day and my desire to see her, and be with her, clearly won the day. So, I didn't know what to do. I just sent up a short prayer and turned my treasured car around and tentatively headed back the way I came. Now I kid you not, a few hundred meters back, there was a 'man' who looked like a farmer standing as if waiting for me, leaning with arms folded, on the front mudguard of a little old beat up looking work utility vehicle. I stopped and he came immediately to my window and asked, "What's the trouble?" I explained the bridge was flooded, that I was on my way to Bundaberg and needed to get there by first thing tomorrow morning for work. I asked him if there was any other way to cross that river. To my great surprise he said "Yes! there is actually. Just a few hundred meters further back on the highway, you'll see a rarely used gravel road off to the left. If you drive down there, you'll come to an old railway bridge. It's not used any more. But if you're very careful you can drive your car up on to it, straddle the old steel railway tracks with your wheels and drive very slowly across. Then you can follow the track to connect back with the main road on the other side. It will be bumpy, but you will be fine." He then returned to his vehicle and drove off! I did exactly as he had said, found it as he had described, and after inspecting that bridge as well as I could in the circumstances, very tentatively drove my precious car across, bump bumping all the way, and got safely home again. I had a good night sleep and awoke fresh for work the next day as if nothing had happened. Now upon reflection, and you too may have noticed some unusual aspects to this situation. That car and man were not there when I had driven at speed up to that flooded bridge just a couple of minutes before! And then he, fortuitously for me, was just there! Following this, after giving me suitable instructions, he immediately disappeared into the night. I also recalled that while there was no starlight or moonlight as I had approached that flooded road bridge, there was in fact a beautiful eerie night light in the sky, when I was inspecting that rail bridge, which lit up the entire structure, so I could see that it looked okay. Otherwise, I may have lacked the courage to cross. I have become convinced that this man was an angel of God who was sent just at the right time to save the day for me. This experience demonstrated the love of God to me at that time, and reinforced my love for Him, encouraging me greatly, and increasing my very real sense that His hand of blessing and protection was strongly on my life.

There was another time I was rounding a corner, at full speed and came upon a large herd of giant cattle all over the road! They seemed to be everywhere. I couldn't see a way through. It was a solid wall of meat, towering higher than my car. So, I just did, in the blink of an eye, what became intuitive. Slammed on the brakes, until I was about to hit the first large beast. Then swerved sharply to the left narrowly missing him and did the same again. Just missing another, and then swung to the first clear space I could 'see'. But I was still operating at speed, because I didn't have enough distance to slow down sufficiently. I did this about six times, zigzagging precariously and miraculously through that massive herd of cattle, which seemed as high as houses, and were just everywhere! Eventually I had reduced to a reasonable speed and was able to negotiate through them slowly and tentatively. When I got through the herd I stopped on the side of the road, shaking like a leaf from head to toe! I waited there for some time. Giving thanks to God for His protection and allowing myself time to recover. I did not hit any of those cattle and the car did not receive any panel damage. Thank you, Jesus! Then, after my poor body returned to some semblance of normality, I drove on towards my destination, reflecting deeply on this amazing event. I wondered how- on-earth I had 'walked' away from this potentially devastating situation largely unscathed. Once again, I could sense the supernatural in this situation. There is no way in a human sense that I could have missed hitting those animals. I was going at open road speed up to this blind corner and came upon them so quickly. There was no way I could have swerved so deftly and sharply at such speed in order to miss this mountain of cattle, which just seemed to be everywhere. It was clearly another miracle. Something was physically assisting the motion of my car, in order to move the way it did, unscathed through that massive obstacle. Once again intervention of the supernatural had occurred into the natural realm, in order to assist me in my circumstances. I then drove on safely to my destination and was able to work normally the next week. However, on rising to the new day, I noticed that every one of my tires had the tread viciously ripped off them, in a multitude of places. Massive bald patches appeared to be everywhere. It was a second miracle that I was able to even drive after that experience. The tyres were in such bad shape, the tyre repair man could not believe his eyes. He did not think it was possible that I had safely and unawares driven such a long distance in the night with the tyres in that condition. He was surprised that some had not blown out! I marvelled yet again at such Divine intervention. It brings a great wave of thankfulness and humility whenever I reflect upon it.

We learned also during these times how difficult it is for a newly engaged couple to avoid sexual intercourse before marriage. This perfectly natural, even supernatural, God-given drive, as mentioned earlier, is so strong, enjoyable and compelling! It is this drive which urges us toward intimacy, ecstasy, connectedness and bonding and which ideally should ensure ongoing satisfaction, delight, love and fulfillment in a marriage relationship. This almost indescribable act of love also makes it possible for most of us to experience the wonderful gift of children, in the course of our life together. We learnt of the delights which come from dreaming about and planning a future new life together. The momentous importance of making a good choice of a life partner was also in the forefront of our minds. For example, I was delighted at my choice of life partner but I think Junie had reservations some times. Partly because she lacked a little confidence in herself about whom she was, her capabilities to face the big challenging world, and some uncertainty regarding the unknown situations that we would have to face as a couple. While I was on the other hand much more confident, but not anywhere near the mature, loving, tender, thoughtful and affectionate husband, which I needed to be to ensure our happiness together. Engagement is where couples explore one another more deeply and more intimately than previously and sometimes this can be a little bit frightening, as well as exciting! But somehow, we got through those ten months of engagement with our relationship still intact. There were times of fun, laughter, delight, sharing, anticipation and increasing intimacy, but there were also times of stress, anxiety, tensions and uncertainty as we tried to manage our long-distance romance as best we could, and do all the necessary planning and activities required as the wedding day approached at great speed. Weddings can be such stressful occasions. But ours went reasonably well.

As I recall again these wonderful and deeply moving memories, I am reminded too that even the wonders of human courtship, engagement and preparing to marry, map amazingly well to the delicate dance of love which also occurs between God, our infinite heavenly Father and Bridegroom, and we frail and delicate human beings! It is most mysterious and wonderful, driven by His compelling desire to have an individual and ultimately close and loving relationship with each of us.

Chapter 8 - The Wedding

Yes, the day eventually did arrive. It was Saturday 27th of May 1972, in the Church of Christ Kingaroy and later at the Country Women's Association (CWA) community hall in the town square. All the longing, dreaming, anticipation, planning and organizing were about to come to fruition, and what a delightful day it was. The organization and events of the day were functional and simple, yet meaningful and beautiful. Seventy-five guests gathered on the day. Many drove long distances to be there; some stayed overnight in town and made a weekend of it. My two best men, who are brothers and close teenage friends of mine, were living in Oakey and Tara at the time. One collected his girlfriend and mum and dad from Tara and drove across. The other came directly from Tara. It was an early afternoon wedding on a balmy, autumn day with blue-white sunny skies, and the winter chill had not yet come. As is often traditional, my dear June and her family and entourage had to bear most of the logistical load of the day. But everything seemed to go like clockwork. There were others more experienced than us who had done it all before, so we just went with the flow as much as we could and used well-established norms. We did as we were asked, went where we were told and said what the minister asked us to say. We knew full well the momentous importance of the occasion and though we were very genuine and sincere in what we were doing, the day seemed to go at lightning speed, with little time to reflect.

We young men were hovering around nervously at the church, awaiting the bridal party for what seemed an eternity. But then they came! We were marshalled quickly into our official places and waited with great anticipation. But of course, then there were photos of the bride's arrival to be taken outside, and the final beautification and arrangement of outfits and such. So we relaxed again and took a breath or two. My two male attendants, who looked extremely handsome, were good friends from my previous church youth group and also played drums and guitar with me in the band we had created in our teens. They and their wives have remained lifelong friends, albeit that they live thousands of kilometres away and we only meet on rare occasions.

Then suddenly, and excitingly, after what seemed like an eternity at the time, the music began to play, and June's lovely, young sisters Jill and Suzie, who were our flower girls, entered confidently. They wore long white dresses with long sleeves, trimmed with the colours of our bridesmaid's outfits, an unusually pretty combination of shades of burgundy. One after another they took their places, followed by the bridesmaid, my sister Judy, and matron-of-honour, June's elder sister Helen, all looking very beautiful in their delightful new outfits.

Having watched the bride's attendants enter gracefully and beautifully and assume their appointed positions at the front of the church, my eyes were now fixed gently but keenly, with an acute level of excitement and anticipation on the front entrance of the church. I felt my heart beat faster, my eyes widen, and I was on the edge of tears. Happy tears of course. This was the time I had been waiting for my whole life! I had no idea how it would feel. My thoughts flashed back to the very first time I had seen this beautiful young maiden, right here in this church, almost exactly where I was now standing. It was at youth group in 1970, and I reflected briefly on the whirlwind of activities which had occurred since. Two years had flashed by, and here I was anxiously awaiting the entrance of my beautiful bride.

Then, she stepped into the room. My heart leapt and my spirit soared. What a treasure. What a beauty. Such a Divine occasion and superb delight. Love, joy, peace, hope, wonder, passion, fulfillment, welled up within my spirit, and that day, I gave every vestige of my heart to this young lady and resolved that I would never stop loving her, and would always remain faithful and committed to her, and the family which we would begin to establish together. That was the day I totally surrendered my heart to her and allowed myself to fall fully in love. She too was making such a priceless and selfless sacrifice, to give herself to me unreservedly on that day. To leave her family, move away from her family home, journey with me into the great unknown, share the rest of her life with me, through good times and through bad, to love me and bear and nurture our children. The very least I could do was give myself fully to her and to her happiness, and with whatever was in my power, to truly love, nurture, honour and keep her all the days of our life together. And this is what I did. In that moment, that sacred instant, as my heart swelled with joy, my spirit was steeled with resolve, as I saw her standing there at the door on that most precious day.

She wore a simple, yet elegant and beautiful, classical, glistening white dress, with a long, transparent overlay, which gave the appearance of a full-length lacey jacket, with sleeves hanging loosely at her delicate wrists, and sides which contrasted the simplicity of the dress and fell the full length of the outfit. Fitted high on her neck, the dress had a relatively high waist which was contoured nicely to accentuate her natural and beautiful curves, and then falling full length to just above the ground exposing the slightest hint of her pretty white shoes. She wore a bonnet of white flowers which curved sweetly around her face and highlighted her raven-black hair and delicate, angelic face. The bridal veil was simple light lace, and the train was medium length, transparent and trailed ethereally a couple of meters behind her. The bouquet consisted of a small, simple delicate arrangement of artificial, white flowers arranged on her tiny, white, wedding Bible and two, long ribbons with embroidered flowers. She was a delight to behold.

Then there were our two beautiful bridesmaids. Helen, two years older than June, was newly married herself and enjoying the delights of her new relationship status. She too, was radiant and with the wonders and experience of new love was an outstanding support and encouragement to her little sister and to me. Judy, my baby sister, had just turned sweet 16, was in the flower of her youth and beauty and came across from Dalby the night before with my mum and dad to have a quick outfit check with the girls and a pre-wedding practice to get us ready for the big day. They both wore long, translucent, burgundy dresses frilled closely to the neck, with loosely fitting sleeves, which belled out at the wrists and a wideband frill of the same material sewn to the bottom of the dress, giving it a more textured and flowing affect. They wore white, flowered bonnets laced with purple ribbon and carried two white flowered balls attached to long purple ribbons. The balls themselves were also woven through with purple ribbon to add colour. Our delightful young flower-girls full of nervous delight at the privilege and spectacle of the occasion, smiled cheekily as they stood up so professionally in their pretty, white outfits, and hair all done up in ringlets and ribbons.

The ceremony went without out a hitch as everyone performed their traditional roles, and June and I committed ourselves to our marriage, in the presence of God and with the support and encouragement of our family and friends. We then took a few minutes to sign the wedding register, and after being introduced as the new Mister and Missus David and June Apelt, greeted the congregation on the way out of the church and assembled briefly out front for further photos, greetings and congratulations. We then went in our wedding cars to a photographic studio close by, where other photos were taken.

Following this, there was a small break until the reception commenced for a mid-afternoon meal and celebration. That was a great family time, prepared generously by the local ladies from our church and with donations and support from family and friends made the cost of the meal and reception very modest.

After experiencing a relaxed and enjoyable time of fellowship over our first meal as a married couple, we had some speeches, cut the cake and took our leave of the group about 5:30 pm, heading to a small motel a short drive down the road, for our first night together. I remember it was such sweet delight to be together

Learning Places: *Real Love*

uninhibited for the very first time as a newly married couple. It truly was worth waiting for. However, having experienced a very full and eventful day after what was such an extremely busy week and month beforehand, we decided to have a beautiful, relaxed night's sleep and delay the extra special delights of our honeymoon until the next day after we arrived at our honeymoon destination in Yeppoon, a small secluded beach-side town just out from Rockhampton, where some wonderful friends had given us free access to their richly appointed holiday house. We had such a wonderful time there discovering the delights of each other, and of new love and intimacy, sexually and relationally, and exploring the manifold adventures of love-making together. This was a profoundly memorable occasion, which set our new love on a strong footing for the surprises, adventures and challenges which we would have to face together.

Apart from having experienced one of the weddings of the year, our wedding weekend was otherwise uneventful in that there were no major problems or disasters which occurred to us or our guests. It had been an election day though, and Joh Bjelke Peterson was greeted there by some of our guests at the local motel where they were staying. This man was the legendary, no-nonsense politician who was Premier of the fine State of Queensland, governing wisely and well for some years, causing it to be one of the most prosperous and enjoyable places to live in Australia.

I should also share that June's little sisters confided in me recently that after the wedding was over, they and their mum had cried their hearts out at the perceived 'loss' of their two big sisters, who were going off to their new married lives. This has not however proved to be the case in that we have always remained close. Though for many years we lived two thousand kilometres apart in Melbourne, Victoria, we always made it a priority, and really enjoyed our family holidays to Queensland where we would spend weeks of quality, family time together. Even though my beautiful wife has died, I still so enjoy family times in Queensland with her family, who have truly become my family. They remain close even in the midst of busy lives, together with my own immediate family with whom I also love to visit. At the time of writing all my children and grandchildren still live close to me in Victoria, as well as others in Queensland and the Northern Territory.

Now in conclusion of this chapter, let me share some further learning from my life, from our wedding, our marriage, and from marriages in general:-

A Marriage including the actual Wedding Ceremony:-

- Is a critically important occasion on the journey of life and has a heavenly as well as earthly dimension.
- Has been a Divinely inspired and encouraged sacrament, in most cultures, since the beginning of humanity.
- Is the ideal way to start a serious relationship where you plan to enjoy sexual intimacy, and there is therefore the possibility or intent of having children.
- Typically includes covenants and vows which create a strong agreement between the man and the

woman. This significantly increases the chances that the marriage and family will remain together. Thus, creating a stronger more stable unit of society and a more positive environment to enjoy life and raise children.
- Seeks to bring together the families of the couple in a positive way, which has potential to increase the strength and viability of the marriage and of our society generally.
- Creates a broader and more diverse web of people who ideally have an interest in making the marriage work and building quality relationships and alliances as a result of the marriage. I know how strongly my life has been enriched and enhanced by the positive alliances of these two clans.
- Includes the concept that most traditional weddings treat vows as being made in the presence of God and this therefore adds weight to the depth of enduring commitment intended in the process.
- Is no more or less effective according to how much or how little money is spent on the occasion! Our wedding was simple, modest and relatively inexpensive, yet very wonderful meaningful and effective in its operation.
- Should not place the bride or groom or their respective families in financial difficulty or debt. This will put the young couple and/or their families in difficult financial stress even before they start out in life. This is not helpful for the future of their relationship.
- Should never, even remotely or indirectly, create the appearance that the bride or the groom is being 'coerced', 'purchased' or 'bribed' in order to take part in the marriage. It should always be a totally

free choice between the man and the woman, preferably based upon mutual love rather than duty or obligation.
- Is much less stressful and far more enjoyable if the couple or their families have saved or given gifts to ensure that the young couple can start their married life together with a reasonable house to live in, appropriate furnishings and no direct or implied net debt.
- Is just the beginning of the marriage journey, and all couples should be given every support and encouragement, by family and society, to make every effort to ensure that they lead a happy fulfilling and successful life together. Love, commitment and enjoyment should ideally be increasing as time goes by, becoming more of an enduring, intimate commitment and unique and special friendship, not just a temporary alliance or convenience.
- Is just a "piece of paper" unless both partners are committed to making an effort to grow in love and stay in love through good times and in not-so-good.

In summary, a marriage has every chance of success and remaining intact for a lifetime of fulfillment and happiness. Contrary to what some with obvious agendas would have you believe, a resounding majority of marriages do last a lifetime. Currently averaging greater than 70%, and in ideal conditions up to 95%, even in these days of sometimes inappropriate liberalization! And the success rate of marriages is actually increasing not decreasing. Divorce rates never ever got anywhere near 50% and on evidence hopefully never will.

The majority of marriages are happy too. Over 80% of currently married couples would typically say they enjoy the experience and would marry the same person again. It is also known that where problems do exist in marriage there are usually very simple yet powerful changes which can be made that will improve the happiness levels significantly. Those same changes when entered into faithfully by both parties will also continue to reduce the divorce rate over time.

The above are all very powerfully beneficial principles issues and characteristics, are typically much more positive than some would have us believe, and when applied well, maximize the chances of success and durability of our marriages and families, thus adding to the quality and satisfaction of life for our whole society.

Nevertheless, the practicalities and direct and indirect costs of those 20+% of family breakdowns, which have occurred for example in the US or in my country Australia, which are only just beginning to be measured... are already proving to be astronomical and devastating to our community and its wellbeing. Would you consider joining with me in seeing what we can do personally and as families, in order to seek to continue to improve this key aspect of our society?

Chapter 9 - Attraction and Healthy Relationships

Having introduced and shared some of the essential elements of marriage, the practicalities, benefits and some flow on effects of its success or otherwise, I would like to take some time to share something else which I have only recently formally observed, and which I have begun to explore in more detail over the last few years. It is the issue that earthly relationships, marriage and family have been given to us since the beginning of humankind as a valuable, socializing and stabilizing covenant as previously described. Yet they have also been given as an earthly example and model of how the relationship between *God* and *Man* is meant to operate, and vice versa! The profound importance of this fact had not occurred to me until a few years ago when I noticed at length a chapter in the Bible which states that this is the case. It is Ephesians chapter five. Another amazing thing about the Bible is that it is so rich with life-changing and enhancing information, one could spend their whole life studying it full-time and not plumb the depth of variety, beauty and wisdom which is contained there-in. Ephesians speaks about many things which could form the contents of many books in their own right, as many other authors have demonstrated. It is well worth a read. However, I will focus on only those aspects which have particularly spoken to me in the context of *Real Love* between brothers and sisters in the Body of Christ, between husband and wife, and between man and God! I hesitate to open up this subject here because it is so large and complex, has been hotly debated throughout history, and since this book does not seek to take a

Bible study approach. It may also seem a little out of the context and flow of my book so far. Nevertheless, these are very important points which are central to the topic of this book.

Ephesians verse twenty-one of chapter five puts forward the command to *submit* to *one another* out of reverence for Christ. This means, for example, deeming others as equals or even better than ourselves. Respecting, loving, honouring and seeking their highest best good, humbly deferring to them, giving them space to be themselves, to express themselves, to belong and to make a contribution. Always being sure to listen carefully to what they have to say, seeking to learn from their wisdom, gifts and experience and faithfully offering to bless, encourage and help them with the needs of life.

Husbands and wives are also meant to submit to each other in this mutually beneficial fashion. However, there is an additional aspect mentioned here which is unique to married couples. It is also commanded that wives should submit to their husbands as the church community is meant to submit to **Christ as the *head* of the church! The Bridegroom!**

Sadly, these verses have been used and abused by numerous people to seek to bring women into a place of feeling or being treated as lesser than or subordinate to men. This has led to all sorts of aberrations in relationships, churches, communities and societies. Nevertheless, because these words are here in this profoundly and uniquely wonderful and authoritative book, one must take them very seriously! However, we should also seek to interpret and implement them in the way that was intended by the Author. The concept of *headship* will always be somewhat of a mystery. In the same way that with God Himself, even though He is personally knowable, lovable and loving, there is always an element of mystery about Him. He has said, unequivocally, that the husband is the *head* of the wife! Why is this so? Why did He make it this way? What did He mean by this? There are so many things we just do not know but let me share at least that which I do know. You may also know other things, and there will always be many unknowns.

God created man and woman of the same material, the same genes and yet He made us different and complementary. The *head* of the body is the part which helps all other parts of the body to work together and has the ultimate arbitration in order to get things coordinated cohesively. This is done by way of brainwaves, nerves, muscles, bones, sinews, tendons and the like. The head also contains the brain and other things which we are yet to fully understand, which connect us to our spirit, and to God Himself, as well as to our body and the world around us... by way of thoughts, feelings, emotions, conscience, imagination, intuition and senses. I want to suggest to you today, that men and women are designed to need each other, and the ultimate in marriage is for them each to surrender to the other so well that they know each other like the back of their own hand, that they connect and communicate with each other so deeply that 'the two really do become *one*', even though they will always remain separate, independent and unique beings. That is the ideal, mutually submissive way that God intended for us to relate in marriage. Conceptually each communicates with the other and with God as if it were through '*one*' mind and '*one*' '*head*'. A classic science fiction mind-meld! A married couple are meant to be operating so closely in unison that they naturally and easily achieve Godly consensus on most issues of life and eternity, and if there ever should be a difference, and there is insufficient time or an unwillingness to resolve it, then the husband will normally have to step up to the mark and make the final call in the interest of maintaining unity and viability of the marriage and family in any given situation. I say normally because in some cases due to for example ill health, mental illness, severe ungodliness, criminal intent, addictive or abusive behaviour, gross immaturity or serious lack of appropriate life skills, the husband will be incapable or ineligible to make a sound decision. In such cases, if she is willing and able, the wife would make the call, or alternatively refer to a trusted and capable adviser or mentor to assist. There can also be cases where the wife will have to assume a form of *headship* for herself and her family because her husband is incapable or unwilling to perform the role effectively. This is also the case for singles, and with single mums, and widows for example... and God fully understands and makes allowance for this type of situation. So in summary, if the husband and wife fully enter into the mystery of the *oneness* which God intended for us, then the *headship* of the husband is actually shared by the wife, in that the two are *one* in spirit. This is the same way which we are meant to operate with God. In that we are so close to Him and so in tune with His heart that we know what we are meant to do or say. But He is always the final arbiter. So even though marital *headship* is somewhat of a mystery, and obviously a challenge to do really well, it is clearly given to teach us humility and how to submit and defer to each other in life, but most importantly to defer to God in all things. It is a mystery, a dilemma, a dichotomy, placed there by our loving God, to force us to reflect on the potentially wonderful, mysterious, beautiful, complex, delightful, peaceful, joyful and fulfilling nature and characteristics of our love relationships with each other, and with Him. This concept is very similar indeed to the account which is also recorded in the Bible regarding Abraham the Father of the Judeo- Christian way of Life. God asked him to sacrifice his son of promise Isaac, whom he had waited for into old age, on an altar on mount Moriah! It is clear that God never intended him to sacrifice his son, but rather that this event would cause the whole world to reflect on what it would mean for a father to sacrifice his son! Which would point to the future event where that is exactly what God our heavenly Father did, when he sent His son, The Lord Jesus Christ here to earth, to die on that terrible cross, for the sins of all humankind. What Wondrous Love! *Real Love!*

Now back to headship. For those who think this heavenly inspired arrangement has given an unfair advantage to the man, consider this! Ephesians Chapter five also says, or implies, that the husband is meant to be a model for his wife, to set an example for her in holiness and righteousness, to love her deeply and as much as he loves himself, to treasure her beyond her wildest imagination, to be her 'saviour', to make her feel and be satisfied and fulfilled in life, to protect her, nurture, love, promote, encourage, equip, enable and release her into her destiny. Always creating a loving and safe environment for her to grow and develop and achieve her fullest potential. The wife is also meant to help her husband grow and develop and succeed in being a good husband by respecting him, honouring and affirming him, in all that is right and good and helping him to grow in areas where he needs to do so. I hope this has made sense. If we are honest with ourselves most women would, even though they may be extremely competent and capable in and of themselves, yearn to have another party to consult with before making big decisions. Likewise, the husband, in and of himself, is usually quite capable and willing to make decisions, but knows that he is inadequate on his own and needs the input and mutual accountability of his partner, in order to make good decisions. And wise husbands and wives together will always know when there is a need to collectively consult with known and wise people outside of their marriage, in order to make high quality decisions or to improve relationship effectiveness or other life- skill areas. However, God should be involved in all decisions in life, especially the larger ones, and should always be the final arbiter. Husband and wife are mutually accountable together but when they join their decision making with God, the all-knowing, all-loving, benevolent and wise Heavenly Father, nothing will stand in their way. They will experience abundant life in all its fullness and their marriage will be delightfully fulfilling to both parties.

I should also say that not all men and women will marry, and some will find themselves 'single' through all manner of life circumstances. Even in these situations this issue still arises, and the bottom line is that every woman needs the ongoing input and sharing of positive male role models in her life, and every man needs the input and sharing of positive females in his life, in order to fully develop and function as men and women. We are meant, with appropriately disciplined, wise, honourable, responsible, compassionate and non-sexual boundaries, to *love* and provide these needs for each other on the journey of life, and particularly within the body of Christ. It is not good to constrain women to only be able to mix socially and relate with women. Neither is it appropriate for men to not have sound and disciplined female friendship and input into their lives. Furthermore, and this may be a little more controversial for some, it is not appropriate or optimally effective for a woman to be only able to socialize with one man in her life, that being her husband. This is unfair, illogical, and unreasonable, and restricts a wife's opportunity to develop fully as a human being. The same goes for men, although they may be less likely to be constrained or inhibited in this matter. Let's leave this topic here for the time being and move on.

These verses in Ephesians express some key concepts very clearly and this discovery has caused me to more closely analyse this stated comparison between earthly and heavenly relationships. There are a number of ways I could have chosen to explore the topic of *Real Love* but the method that seemed to make most sense to me was to identify and analyse the various stages of earthly love, between a man and a woman, which I have been progressively unfolding through my own love story here in this book. Let me now share some of the relationship elements and mechanisms that I have identified thus far, for the purpose of illustration, and to seek to map each one to the perceived stages and elements of love between man and God.

I should also state at this point that the concepts, stages

and comparisons described here are ideals and often seem difficult to comply with. In the interest of simplicity, I will explore and describe the models here in their pure and ideal form before commenting later, on the more challenging aspects of relationships, both earthly, and heavenly.

Indicative parallel stages are:-

The Basic Drive for Relationship -

Firstly, there is a strong foundational and natural drive, inherent and observable in humans, which both consciously and unconsciously urges us to seek out and acquire friends and associates for the purpose of giving and receiving love, acceptance, security, comfort and mutual benefit... and then optionally, potentially and ultimately to find a mate for procreation, and the extension of humankind.

Earthly: This drive is an inner compulsion toward seeking genuine relationship, affection, love and belonging. It compels and assists us toward building strong friendships, groups, communities, churches and families. The foundational, healthy and safe level of this love does not require a sexual dimension, and although that aspect is an ever-present facet of human relationship chemistry, it is not a prerequisite, and in fact is not recommended, or needed, in order to achieve and enjoy optimal fulfilling and enduring, strong healthy friendships and relationships in life.

Heavenly: This earthly, natural human drive mirrors the heavenly, supernatural, spiritual drive which is also inherent in each one of us and causes us to seek out relationship, love and belonging with God himself. This basic level of human love mirrors the first level of love which we can have with God, and is explored, deepened and developed in similar ways to how we develop a deep and meaningful relationship with other earthly friends.

All basic relationships, be they heavenly or earthly, require for example spending time with each other, talking, sharing, listening, taking an interest in each other's thoughts, ideas, needs, goals and dreams, and generally seeking to get to know each other better. Furthermore, experiencing such genuine basic friendship in this world and with our heavenly Father is something which we all need, and inherently desire, in order to be totally satisfied and fulfilled. It helps us to experience true happiness, peace and love. On the flip side, if we are not able, or allowed, to build and enjoy these types of quality relationships, we will more than likely experience or be tangibly affected by a really serious practical, emotional and spiritual lack. Sadly, this can then lead to all manner of problems, many of which are quite serious.

Some such examples can be:-

- an inability to effectively relate to people generally or to men, women, fathers or mothers specifically
- inability to relate to God because of a poor relationship with a father
- difficulty in believing that one is worthy of forgiveness or love, even the love of the Lord Jesus
- anger about the fact that one has not received adequate love
- difficulty in loving others because of the lack of

- love received
- hardness of heart developed as a protection mechanism
- confusion related to 'self' or 'other' and relationship boundaries
- substance addiction through loneliness, emptiness and lack of purpose
- a sense of rejection and a wounded or offended heart... and so on!

As you can see, these are non-trivial issues and actually describe a large portion of the social and psychological challenges which we struggle with as a society. Building healthy relationships and being able to effectively give and receive love really do make the world a better place.

The Deeper Observation and Attraction Phenomenon-

In addition to and as an overlay or complement to the above-mentioned basic, foundational drive to seek out love and connection, there are also a myriad of other multi-facetted more mysterious *observation* and *attraction* processes which occur in relationships... These are phenomena, characteristics and issues which we are only just beginning to discover, explore and understand at a more detailed level.

Now, notwithstanding the possibility of being proved wrong in some minor points, by future research and the passing of time, I am going to seek herewith to explore and describe some of these various aspects from my own life discoveries and experience to date.

From an earthly and a heavenly perspective many of the aspects of this inter-human male—female observation and attraction phenomenon can be basically described by referring to them under the headings of the different senses with which we have been endowed. One of the major observation and attraction senses is sight. This gift is a manifold and wondrous ability given as a creative blessing to most people. One could write thousands of books about it and the other senses with which we have been blessed, but my focus here is to refer only, and albeit briefly, to the sense of sight and its involvement as part of the observation and attraction process which occurs between man and woman and with God.

Let's proceed:-

Sight

Earthly: - The things we see with our physical eyes can be felt, deduced or subjectively observed to be beautiful, worthy of admiration, attractive, unattractive, neutral or a myriad of other stages in between. Some of these observations are learned, through good or not so good teaching, observation or experience in life, but some are inherently just a part of who and what we are. For example, when a man *sees* a beautiful woman, what does he typically deem to be beautiful? Is it her warm delightful smile? Her sparkling blue eyes, her satin-like long blonde hair, or delicately contoured, warm and inviting face? Her just-right cute little ears, elegantly styled lips, pearly white teeth, her tiny pixie nose, long slender neck, squared yet rounded ballerina shoulders or indeed her cleavage and related generous or appropriately adequate endowments! What is it about her arms, hands, fingers, nails, milky white skin, curves, contours, waist, hips, legs, ankles, feet, toes etc? What is it that he first notices? Or is it all of the above and more! Alternatively, or in addition, it may be the way she walks; the elegance and grace with which she carries herself; the cute way that she tosses her hair, her personal confidence or indeed her seemingly delicate shyness? Then there is her outfit. Tops, bottoms, dresses, pants, tights, shoes, colours, cuts and styles, loose and fitted, boldly or cheekily exposing certain parts and discretely or teasingly hiding or partly hiding others... and so on. There is no end to what a woman can do to display or enhance her natural beauty. And there are also many other unique distinct and wonderful aspects to a woman, a true marvel of creation! I think you are getting the idea! and this is obviously just the beginning.

We would doubtless each have a view on what we thought / felt were the most beautiful aspects of this lady and our opinions are often very different one from another. We all seem to be designed to experience observation, attraction and delight through different forms and aspects of nature. And yes, we do all 'see', we cannot avoid 'noticing', and if we took the time, we would all have a view on what we thought were her most beautiful features. My learning by the way in this matter is that there is something beautiful in all of us, both male and female. Sometimes however, voluntarily or involuntarily we attempt to keep this beauty hidden within ourselves and we can also for many reasons be reticent or find it difficult, to allow ourselves to see beauty in others.

Now a slightly different but related question. What aspects did you observe, or feel, were beautiful, verses those which you found attractive? Here's lies a mystery! I'm not going to explore this topic exhaustively, as some might wish, but simply to a level necessary for highlighting and thinking about the processes of *observation* and *attraction*... In order to acquire a deeper general understanding, to discover how they actually factor into the numerous elements of natural human love and relationships and to explore how this knowledge might help with considering appropriate boundaries. This will also hopefully give us a better and deeper revelation regarding our relationship with God.

There is a definite boundary, and a different level of intensity and preoccupation, between *observing* that someone or some aspect of a person is beautiful, and that of being, or allowing ourselves to become more deeply *attracted* to the person. One is a rational and/or intuitive process of simply acknowledging the beauty. The next could be for example a genuine level of thoughtful admiration, which means to regard with wonder and affirmation. Both of these processes are entirely appropriate in a normal healthy safe and positive relationship between any man and woman in a wise prudent and civil society. *Beyond this place however*, a heightened more mysterious and less definable process begins, which by way of the man's own inner workings and that of the woman being admired, begin to create an environment, which for simplicity, I will refer to as *attraction*. This by definition, could be for example, a feeling that you would like to consider the possibility of having a deeper more serious and maybe even ultimately intimate relationship one with the other. This is the very clear boundary between a loving friendship, which we should all be able to maintain with each other and the beginnings of a relationship of intimate dimensions.

This is the point at which wise and conscious thoughtfulness and decisions need to be made. Indeed, one should ideally give thought to this issue much earlier if you even vaguely suspect that there is ever going to be a possibility of you perhaps feeling that you might like to take this relationship further. My life-learning is that it is best to think about these issues long before this point is reached. If you consider there is even a remote probability that you might feel this way, it is most wise to reflect carefully on the type of relationship that is appropriate and right, with this particular person and in their current circumstances... and then thoughtfully manage the relationship accordingly. If you believe you may like to consider a deeper relationship, that should be first explored in theory within yourself personally, and with God, and then if and when the time seems right, with the other party, in a low-key fashion, before you ever seriously consider the possibility of allowing yourself to emotionally engage more deeply.

This is also the point at which some people would describe that we may begin to *fall in love*. A powerful phrase, but it is a very real phenomenon which we all need to deal with, ideally in advance of it happening. This intoxicating state of being, involves all manner of spiritual, mental, physical, emotional and hormonal chemistry, which once unleashed is difficult to contain, and can be devastating to the parties involved, particularly if the relationship does not eventually blossom into the safe, loving, intimacy and permanency of a covenant marriage. Its far better to look at any relationship in advance of allowing the possibility of such happening. This is also called self-control, and this boundary can be referred to as the battle ground of the mind. It actually forms a very real part of the frontier of the cataclysmic conflict between light and darkness in our world. It is the point at which we can make really good sound decisions, or alternatively all sorts of painful relational aberrations can and do occur, over and over again, in our society, often due to lack of information or experience, or indeed just selfish wilfulness, putting ourselves and our own passions, desires and wants before the welfare of others, even that of ourselves... and it so often turns out badly, if not managed well! So, I am sure that as a thoughtful and concerned reader you would agree, that in the best interest of society generally and the individuals involved, this type of serious deeply passionate, loving and intoxicating relationship should ideally only be seriously explored, if the couple is prepared to consider the possibility of covenant marriage. We all need to be open to talking about and practically dealing with these types of issues in order to build healthy loving community relationships.

I'm sure by now you have observed that in this book I am predominantly exploring the man's feelings and experiences in relation to the woman. This is both for expedience and because I can confidently and authoritatively speak on this subject. I am hopeful that my female readers will find these male oriented perspectives, feelings, experiences and reflections interesting and helpful and I am also confident that if you are a woman, you will be eminently able to comfortably and capably compare, contrast, complement, deduce, reflect and extrapolate from the man's experiences, that which you as a woman do or could be feeling or experiencing in the same type of moment and context. I trust this is a fair assumption.

Heavenly: - From a heavenly relationship perspective what we see with our physical eyes can also prompt us to sense, deduce or subjectively observe some aspect of heaven, of God Himself, or our relationship with Him. Take a simple example of you observing a tree. This is the most beautiful tall strong vibrantly green tree you have ever seen. It has caught your attention because of it tallness, its strength in face of a strong prevailing wind, the way its strong branches reach out symmetrically in all directions, providing balance to the tree and perching and nesting places for the birds of the air, as well as affording shelter and shade for the creatures which gather at its base. Even though it is summer, and the grass has become dry through the relentless rays of seasonal sun, this beautiful tree remains tall, green and resilient, drawing sustenance from the streams of hidden water, flowing and in plentiful reservoirs, richly occurring beneath this broad undulating and fertile land. This is the earthly visual encounter of sensing, deducing and observing that which is marvellous and beautiful about this tree. And now you begin to regard it with wonder and affirmation, as you celebrate what you are seeing and the implications of its beauty and presence in this world. Then, if you will allow or indeed encourage it to occur, something begins to happen *beyond this place!* As you observe the awesome wonder of this simple yet profound phenomenon of a tree you begin to reflect upon the order, creativity, elegance, variety, thoughtfulness, synergy, provision and, dare I say it, design! For it is not reasonable to pontificate that it could have happened by chance no matter how many eons you might like to hypothesize. It is in fact quite reasonable and logical to assume that there is a creator and designer involved, and that the beauty of this tree and the circumstances of its presence here in this environment, speak of a higher more advanced attractive and infinitely capable entity, one which you may indeed seek to discover and to get to know more closely.

Now we need to return to my original exploration regarding the observation of beauty, followed by deeper attraction between a man and a woman, because contrary to the opinion of some, one cannot have a personal and intimate relationship with a tree. A man may however experience a delightful and wonderfully intimate relationship with a woman, and she with him, which is normally referred to as marriage, and so too may a person have an intimate and committed relationship with God. We have already begun to share the complexity and variety of connections and issues which occur between a man and a woman in a normal healthy community relationship, and even more so in a covenant marriage. So too is the potential richness of relationship that we can have with God, since we are clearly made in His image, and He desires to have a personal relationship with us. Finally, while in an earthly sense we are best to focus our deeply intimate passions and affections on just one chosen marriage partner, so too in the case of our relationship with God, we inherently need and should also always explore a deeper, more intimate and purposeful relationship with

Him alone. For there is only one true and Living God as discovered and described in my earlier books, and we can always get to know Him better. One can never get too close to God, and there is always more to know about Him than we will ever have time to discover!

Continuing to briefly explore the various senses in relationship to observation and attraction we now come to hearing.

Hearing

Earthly: - Have you experienced how the voice of a person can be music to your ears, catching your attention when you hear it... and sweet to the emotions... invoking all sorts of memories, positive feelings, affirmation and possibilities. Perhaps revealing a person with whom you'd really like to talk further. There is also the way in which certain music brings beautiful emotions to the fore. In my case the voice of my lovely wife June was music to my ears. It was always a joy to hear her speaking, singing, laughing, sharing and bantering contentedly on the innumerable issues of life and love. When someone you love deeply, dies, you seriously realize even more so, the wonders of voice and hearing. How together they make meaningful helpful connections between people and how much you miss that sound. Recently I had a very notable and emotional experience where one of Junie's sisters spoke behind me from another room. Just a short phrase, but the resonance of her voice at that moment struck a wonderful memory, because it sounded exactly like my Junie's voice. After many years I thought I had forgotten her voice, but it is there written on my heart, and hearing and memories, for all time. She had a gift of music too and this gift was also life giving to me. Hearing forms the foundation of interpersonal and community relationships and is pivotal to experiencing the joys of casual relationships and friendships, as well as a deeper and more wonderfully intimate relationship with a marriage partner. The more you love a person the more you will enjoy hearing their voice.

Heavenly: - The same applies in the heavenly realm and in a relationship with God. He is always speaking to us. Yearning deeply to dialog with us and share the journey of our lives. But sometimes we struggle to hear, or indeed can't hear Him for some reason. My experience and that of many others whom I know has been that if we really want to hear from God, we need to have a heart to learn from what He says... and a willingness to do what He asks us to do. For example, to say "Dear Lord Jesus, speak to me Lord and I will follow you all the days of my life and do what you ask me to do". Then say "Lord I'm listening right now what is it that you would like to say to me today. What would you have me do today, and what of my life and future together with you." Then assuming that the message is positive and constructive, which it usually is, trust that the first idea and thought which comes to mind is from Him and begin to take it seriously and do what He says. He will speak with us every time we give Him opportunity, if we take what He says seriously. He knows when we are genuine. Then begin to look for Him everywhere we go, in everything we do, and we will begin to sense Him, and know what He's up to. We will begin to hear Him more regularly, giving us ideas, observations and instructions. Ask Him to make our thoughts His thoughts and His thoughts our thoughts that we might have the Mind of Christ on all matters! I have heard 'voices' which sound so sweet and melodic to the ear that I turn my head to see who spoke and sometimes am surprised whose voice it was. Sometimes it is the voice of God, sometimes a person whom God wants us to pay attention to. Other voices just sound normal, some grate on you, some are just bearable. But I have found that if you have a problem with someone's voice there is usually an issue which needs attention, either with yourself, or with them, or both. It is wise to pray and seek The Lord about what to do about such situations. Repentance, forgiveness, inner healing, reconciliation and restoration are always critical for a full recovery, and always remember that the tongue can be like a raging fire, a dangerous sword or a deadly poison, if used wrongly. Our words matter and they can create and build up or destroy and tear down. Every word we speak is recorded for all time in the ether and sound waves of our universe and often in the memories of our hearers as well. Let our tongues always be under the control or our minds, and our minds under God's control, governed by our close, understanding and intimate relationship with Him, so that we may always know what to say, or not say, in every situation. That our speech is seasoned with salt, sweet like honey, gracious, healing, constructive and helpful to all. You know, God says in His amazing and timeless miraculous book the Bible, that when we become His friends, which is entirely possible and open to all, through acceptance of what Jesus did for us on the Cross of Calvary... that He will give us wisdom for life and share with us in a needful and timely way, his innermost thoughts and intentions, in every situation in which we find ourselves. What a wonderful blessing!

Smell

Earthly - I'm sure you've experienced the tantalizing fragrance of something beautiful in nature. My sense of smell is not very acute, so I don't notice a lot of scents. However, I have sufficient sense of smell to enjoy life to the full and most of the wonderful fragrances of God's creation. A smell can trigger a memory just like a song. Pepperina tree scent always reminds me of primary school where we had many such trees growing in the school grounds. I don't enjoy the smell of many perfumes because they are too strong, intrusive even sometimes cause an allergic reaction. But there was one my wife June wore called Youth Dew. It is just another reminder of her, and the love we had for each other. When she wore it the delicate scent always gave me a sense of intimate peace contentment romance and enjoyment while going out on special occasions with her, and it was always a discreetly elegant and subtle background scent in our bedroom. Sense of smell is a big part of life. It comes into so many situations good and bad and can alert that something needs attention, invite an initial observation, or ultimately be an aid to attraction and intimacy. But it's not just about manufactured fragrances. We all have our own natural scents which vary person to person and can heighten observation and attraction. They are elementally involved in courting, dating, falling in love, and in the most deeply intimate forms of lovemaking. What a beautiful gift from God the sense of smell and the unique and personal scents which he gives each one of us.

Heavenly - Fragrance is a wonderful part of God's creation and the ability to smell is a gift from him to human beings made in His image. There seems to be an infinite number of fragrances which he has made. Every naturally occurring fragrance seems to have meaning and purpose. Some are to attract insects which will pollinate the flowers so the plant can reproduce. Others to induce the desire for love making to preserve humankind and all forms of life on earth. Some are just for simple enjoyment of onlookers. I have recently had experiences also where I can sense the presence of God in worship or in ministry through what appears like a fragrance or a sense of a fragrance. It's hard to tell whether it's a real scent or a spiritual scent and to what degree one can 'smell' it verses 'know' it. Other friends, probably the ones who have an acute sense of smell, often smell a strong sweet fragrance when God is present, and it seems to be a real scent in the human dimension but made up of uniquely heavenly elements. So, God also uses scent in our relationship with Him as well. To alert us to His presence, soothe or minister to our spirit, increase our enjoyment in being with Him, highlight something He wants to point out to us, bring something to our attention, or give us some form of understanding or instruction. For example, I can often smell demons or the presence of evil which always prompts me to cleanse the environment I am in with the Blood of The Lord Jesus and The Power of His Name! I encourage each one of us to watch carefully for fragrances in our dealings with God, and in our growing love relationship with Him, because He earnestly desires to make meaningful and loving connections with each and every one of us in life and in eternity. In our earthly and heavenly relationships, it's always wise to be alert to the presence and nature of smells and fragrances, with a view to enjoying God to the maximum potential of His creation, as well as fully understanding the environment in which we find ourselves. This will help us in avoiding or averting any unwanted, unwise, undesirable, dangerous or destructive activities and responses which people or indeed spirits may be trying to engineer to achieve inappropriate outcomes. As well as taking full advantage of the Divine appointments and opportunities which God brings across our paths every day.

Touch

Earthly - This is one of the most fascinating senses. I don't know what I'd do without it. In a recently written book, an author coined the idea that touch was in fact a love language, of which he had discovered five. I feel there are actually more than this, but his treatise was helpful and convincing, touch certainly is a key element of love between humans, and also involved in many other synergistic relationships in nature. Since my wife died seven years ago, I have become an expert on this subject. In a loving satisfying and fulfilling marriage relationship, there is, or should always be, copious amounts and forms of touch. From friendly and innocent, to cheeky and flirty, right up to the most intimate loving and sensually exhilarating forms! However, when a partner dies, in addition to all the other issues of grief, loss, trauma, sadness, loneliness, change- shock, increasing workloads and such, which have to be dealt with, one also experiences what I call a massive 'touch deficit'. Often this is not detected immediately, and without remedy can have lots of negative flow-on effects, as do the other above-mentioned conditions. Everyone needs an adequate level of human touch in their life whether married or not, and one of the theses of this book is that it is appropriate, even mandatory, for all individuals to experience a reasonable level of interpersonal, safe, non- sexual touch, in the course of their normal daily lives, in order to enjoy a balanced, healthy and happy lifestyle. I have learned too that the most practical helpful and appropriate forms of this touch, are for example a warm gentle but firm handshake, an encouraging hand on the shoulder or around the shoulders, taking hold of an arm or a hand and adding an encouraging word, an affirming pat on the back, a kiss on the cheek when culturally appropriate, and the most beneficial of all... The Almighty Hug! You have no idea how important a hug can be to a person going through most types of painful life experiences and emotions. For me this element of touch has been and remains a key element in my recovery from the loss of my wonderful wife. The other two keys are to talk about my loss and related feelings whenever I need to, and to cry whenever I need to, even in the presence of company. In conclusion, I'm sure you've heard that a new baby if denied regular warm encouraging hugs, love, attention and affirmation will often actually die because of this deficit, even if they have sufficient nutrients. Touch is a radically important element of our lives.

Heavenly - This form of ethereal touch is a little more difficult to define. My experience however is that in the midst of the most difficult and challenging life circumstances a 'touch' from The Lord is the most powerful and helpful remedy. Human touch in these times as described above is also paramount, but that *heavenly* 'touch' goes beyond anything one can experience with flesh and blood. Although having said this, I have found that folk who walk closely with God and have surrendered their heart to him, can also deliver a form of *heavenly* touch through the action of God's Holy Spirit, in and through their own human touch. An example of heavenly touch which comes readily to mind is that many years ago I experienced a powerfully traumatic diving accident, described in more detail in one of my earlier books. After the incident I had somehow dragged myself up to my feet, and dazed but miraculously totally uninjured, walked tentatively back to the seashore. As I went, I sensed the presence of God, His tender, healing, soothing touch was upon me, and this amazingly beautiful calmness and comfort swept over me. This served to reduce the level and effects of the massive shock and trauma and eased me back into reality. To this day this 'touch' of God reminds me of His presence, love and provision.

On another much more shocking occasion, in fading light Friday afternoon after a long and very busy week, while leaving work to drive home to spend time with my beloved, a sad and troubled young man darted crazily out from where he had been concealed behind a tree on the median strip, directly into the path of my oncoming car. He was killed instantly and thrown ten meters down the road ahead, because I had no time to stop before the impact. You can imagine my terrible shock! The deadening thud and the body flying violently through the air! Not realizing at the time that it was a human being! For I had hit kangaroos like this before.

However, even in the midst of that extreme trauma, as I planted both feet on the brakes and screeched to a halt, got sheepishly out of my car, walked feebly toward the body lying lifelessly on the ground... And suddenly realized with a violent shock that this was a man! And not an animal! Miraculously, I still sensed that calming touch of God, His comforting arms were around my shoulders, and I felt His supernatural peace flood over me and into my heart. It was as if He was right there with me organizing things to minimize my pain, trauma and shock. Because you can imagine what might have happened if I had been accused of manslaughter or negligent driving! Immediately then, while my mind was darting around deciding what I should do, the driver of a large Road Truck, which had been following closely on my left, was at my side, put his hand on my shoulder and said, "I will be your witness, it was not your fault". Police and ambulance were there in minutes as if they knew it was going to happen. A kindly police officer then came up to me, put his hand on my shoulder and said, "Are you okay?" I responded that I thought I would be! He then said in quick succession. "He is dead! We'll have to impound your car! Come down to the police station tomorrow morning and give us your statement!" and "Have you got anybody to take you home?" That was a hard question since I had only been working in that town a few weeks. Yet immediately he asked that question a beautiful young lady who worked with me, was there at my side, took me by the arm and said, "Come to my place and I'll take you home in a little while." It was all over in just a few short minutes. A sweet and gentle, caring, young lady, she drove me to her house and she and her family proceeded to debrief with me and comfort me for an hour or so. Then many copious hugs and encouragements later, as promised, she took me back to where I was staying. I would love to meet that kind and delightful young lady again one day, to thank her for her kindness and tell her how much it meant to me. She had a very unusual name which I think might have been Leneave. The boys and girl at the share-rental house where I was staying were surprised to see me and wanted to hear all the stories again, which made for a very late night. I had trouble getting to sleep that night thinking through what I needed to say and what might happen... And of course, the question came "Why me, Lord?" That's when I felt his hand on my shoulder again, as I lay there troubled in my bed, as He quietly said, "Better you than someone else who does not have my peace on their life." This settled my spirit immediately and I drifted into a peaceful sleep and rose and did my duty at the police station next day. Quite timidly at first, and feeling uncertain as to what it might mean, I advised the police sergeant that I believed he had done it on purpose. He then said, "Don't say any more, just give us your statement as it happened, and we can talk later." So, after taking my statement the police officer had me sign the document, and advised me that I was correct, he had a suicide note in his jacket pocket. While making me very sad for him, this gave me a great deal of peace, that I had done nothing wrong, and could expect no negative repercussions as a result of this accident.

There are many other powerful examples of the touch of God in my life, but these will do to demonstrate the point. Touch is a critical dimension to human life and its absence can be devastating. I have seen men and women who have lost a partner, rush into a new relationship, simply because of this touch deficit, the desire for sexual intimacy, the perceived 'need' to have someone... or alternatively even because of the need to be 'needed'! I have learned it is best to wait a long, wise, thoughtful and prudent time before considering remarriage after the loss of a partner. Also, that if there is insufficient loving touch in our marriage relationship, this is a very real and important issue which deserves focused attention... And it isn't always just the lack of sexual touch that is at issue... but sexual intimacy is extremely important in a covenant marriage relationship. Remembering also that as stated above there is a clear boundary between touch that is appropriate in the general community and that which is ideally meant to operate only in the safety, intimacy and privacy of marriage. I don't think I need to expand further on this topic because I believe most of us inherently know the type of touch which would be deemed to be untoward or offensive. If we don't happen to know this, then we should consult with an appropriate wise and trusted friend or professional. I should also say here that I have observed that inappropriate touch, affairs, liaisons, etc are extremely destructive to society, families, friendships, communities, workplaces and to marriages... whether conducted in private or in public... even if our partner never finds out. As soon as we embark upon such behaviour, we immediately demean ourselves, and are also taking advantage of the other party. This is not recommended in a positive and healthy society... and we all so need and yearn for a healthy, safe, peaceful, loving, honouring community and nation in which to live. An understanding and mutual agreement needs to exist between both parties before advancing any relationship in the area of touch... and there are also many other practical, rational, sensible, thoughtful, moral, emotional and often legal implications to be considered as well.

Taste

Earthly - Taste too is a fascinating thing. Apparently, every person tastes a particular substance slightly differently due our physical and emotional makeup, and DNA. Tastes trigger emotions, bring back memories, excite hormones, prompt positive and negative feelings and so on. A master chef has all manner of wonders at his/her disposal in order to tempt the taste buds and heighten the emotions. Meals are powerful and beneficial in initiating new relationships, building and maintaining community, and making covenant. Meals have been used to celebrate, to commiserate, to build alliances, cajole, bribe and negotiate. Dates entered into by potential new lovers nearly always include the element of food and taste. Food has always been a key part of romantic relationships since the dawn of time, and rightly so. This gift of taste is worth exploring routinely as part of our normal healthy community relationships and also in the more intimate contexts of our marriage relationships. There is an element of truth in the saying that the way to a man's heart is through his stomach! And it can work just as well with the ladies, once you discover what they like. Caution is advised though in that gluttony really is a sin and a very unhelpful companion on the journey of life. Thus, wasting resources, ruining health, breaking up families and so on. All things should be done in moderation. However, there are also substances which can induce hallucination, out of body experiences, euphoria, heightened sexual pleasure and propensity, and so on. These substances and *tastes* should be avoided altogether in the best interest of a healthy life, marriage, family, community and society. Our society encourages freedom, but this type of freedom destroys lives and souls, marriages and families, and most of them are powerfully compelling and addictive as well, making it almost impossible to stop once one has started.

Heavenly - Taste like all senses is heavenly in the sense that they have been provided by a compassionate and loving creator God, who wants this world in which we live to be enjoyable and delightful. The very phenomenon of taste is itself ethereal and heavenly, in that our spirit can by way of our body, and all its wondrous makeup, brain, nerves, cells, saliva, taste buds, emotions, hormones and the like, miraculously experience the wonders of taste. It is also possible to taste the presence of God, and of evil, and this is different for every person as well... but important in making wise decisions on the journey of life. Taste and smell are closely allied. Often one can smell, as well as taste, in the same instant of time, and the two senses work together to complement one another. So if you taste/smell the presence of evil. There are only two real choices... Get the hell out of there! Or alternatively, cleanse the place of evil, in all its forms, through the power and presence of God, and the blood of the Lord Jesus Christ. Then invite His glory and healing to bring revival and restoration, to all people who have been deceived by the evil, so that this location may become a fountain-head of His glory. Hallelujah! I have seen this happen many times. So when I am prompted to do it, I just do it, and leave the outcomes up to God! And time and time again I hear powerful testimonies of how things have changed.

Taste is important in spiritual discernment, and communication with God and with men and women, and can refine and enhance our love relationships. Just as it is worth the effort in refining and tuning our ability to hear from God, it is also worth working with Him to enhance our communication through the medium of taste. It was very beneficial to me recently as I was exploring a new country for Jesus, and seeking out how to discover its needs and issues, in order that I might better pray and declare His words, over the various people, locations and situations of the land. The sense of taste in combination with smell alerted me to the presence of demons and evils and evil intentions, and I was thus able, together with friends, to thwart the enemy's plans and take territory from him in the powerful name of The Lord Jesus Christ. This too is part of what He means for us to do when He says, "Go and make disciples of all Nations". There is an aspect that disciples need to be made one by one, but we can also disciple Nations. By strategically addressing, engaging and influencing all different levels and domains of society, as well as by just declaring and doing daily that which the Lord asks us to do... and encouraging others to do likewise.

Sixth Sense - Intuitively Being Aware of the 'Unseen'

Sixth Sense was illustrated to a degree in a movie of the same name a few years ago. This sense however is not just about seeing dead people. Not many people actually see dead people as depicted in this movie, however many of us have had a glimpse of a loved one who has died who wishes to say goodbye, or inherently seems to know that you need to say goodbye. It is an opportunity to say parting words of love and making peace before they head off to glory.

Sixth Sense has also had bad press over the years in that people who experience it vividly have sometimes been deemed to have psychiatric problems. Our often said to be 'rational', 'logical', 'scientific', 'existential' forms of education and lifestyle have also downplayed or denigrated this additional not well understood sense. This is often done consciously and purposefully to avoid acknowledgement of the reality of God, ignore the possibility of having a relationship with Him, and to deny the existence of other spiritual dimensions. Worse still it has been used by some as a mechanism to try to condition society toward an anti-Christian and anti-God worldview. This is much more serious and could well be described as a form of systemic abuse, in that knowledge which is critically important for human beings to know about, and to experience from a very young age, in order to live a balanced and healthy life, has been intentionally and pervasively withheld. Our western societies have suffered greatly under this problem, and we are beginning to 'reap the whirlwind' of living life without sound values and a viable worldview, or alternatively, with skewed ones which are often unfounded, untrue, unworkable and proving very destructive to our society.

Earthly - From an earthly perspective it is important to be aware of, be positive about and to consciously develop our capabilities in this area. This sixth sense allows us to overlay a spiritual dimension to our physical senses. In fact, the *heavenly* subheadings under each sense category above have included descriptions of exactly this phenomenon. 6th sense allows us at appropriate times, and it would seem according to higher Divine purposes, to see what is not visible to the human eye, hear what is not physically audible, smell that which is not in this dimension, touch or be touched by what is not visible, taste what is not physically there, and know that which is not knowable by the action of the other five senses. I have already given examples above of how this can occur in the course of our human lives and indicated that these gifts, skills and talents can be developed here in this world.

You can see how the overlay of this sixth element on our other normal physical senses can serve to enhance and deepen our relationships one with the other. This sixth sense can enhance normal human friendships, family and community relationships to an extremely enjoyable and mutually satisfying, beneficial and productive level. It can potentially also take an earthly marriage from being a very mediocre relationship on to being the most on fire, passionate, loving, honouring, fulfilling, satisfying relationship that a man and a woman can possibly experience during this earthly existence.

Heavenly - There is a problem, however. This sense heightens our five physical senses to be more spiritual in their function and puts us in contact with our spiritual self. That is our own soul and spirit. The entity which is our personality, that which is 'me', the 'one', which is self-aware and seeking to survive as a human being, in this physical body and in this material world. It is that which helps put us in touch with the invisible spiritual part of who we are. This sense also serves to make us more aware of the other spiritual dimensions, beings and agendas going on around us. The problem is this. A sixth sense in its raw natural unredeemed form, just like the other five senses, in and of themselves, embody no sense of discernment, no ability to know right from wrong and no discretion or wisdom. When naive and ill-informed the sixth sense can do great damage to a person in all aspects of their personality.

You see, the effective operation of the sixth sense is entirely dependent on the proper and efficient operation of the Seventh Sense. There are so many out there in our community, often in total innocence and good intentions, seeking to help people get in touch with and activate their sixth sense, yet do not have the skills or inherent spirituality to lead people in to Seventh Sense!

Seventh Sense - Intimate 'Knowing' of the Seen and the Unseen

Had you discovered this before? I became aware of the concept of the sixth sense long ago. But it never seemed enough! The sixth sense did not fully explain, nor did it go far enough to solve the world's real problems. In fact, it can make them so much worse. When a person is exposed to the spiritual dimension which surrounds us here on earth, there is a violent war going on between good and evil, and evil's intention is to kill, steal and destroy all that is good. So, opening up a human being to become spiritually aware of this ether-world, by way of an undiscerning sixth sense, actually can make things worse than before. Better to be naïve and disengaged... then to engage directly, tangibly and unprepared, with the very forces of darkness... which seek to deceive, mislead, lie to, and annihilate humankind... By whatever means they can. Some of which you see clearly operating in our tangible world today.

Earthly: - The seventh sense lies dormant and atrophied in every human being from birth and can only be effectively activated by one means. We need to **acknowledge** that in our own human strength, unaided by God Himself, we are unable to survive effectively in this world and achieve all that we are destined to do... And that our abilities and faculties, physical and spiritual, are severely limited, constrained and prone to error and self-interest. We need to **seriously repent** and show remorse for all past activities, motives, attitudes and intentions which have been unhelpful, destructive and not in any way good, or of God. Even of our own feeble attempts to do what we thought was worthwhile and good, in our own views, opinions, strength and capabilities. We need to **accept** with gratitude and thanks the **offering that Jesus made** for us on the Cross of Calvary in Jerusalem 2000 years ago, where He took all of our sins upon Himself and suffered the indignity of going to hell for it... then by His sovereign power overcame sin and death and rose again... first in His mortal body to demonstrate the reality of His victory here in time and space, then went on 40 days later to ascend into heaven from which He came. Then it's important to **invite Him** into our lives **to be Lord** of all and everything we do and **invite Holy Spirit** of God into our lives to activate our spirit, renew and purify our souls and to **ignite the seventh sense** within us. This is so that we can commune with God in loving, selfless, complete, vulnerable and total abandonment and intimacy... The same way in principle that a new bride and bridegroom commit to each other at their wedding and on their wedding night.

This act of faith in God and of The Lord Jesus Christ unites our spirit with God's Spirit, connects our heart with His and our mind with His mind in a wonderful intimate way. Just like earthly marriage. He knows us intimately and we have the potential to know Him in the same way. We are vulnerable to Him, yet we feel safe and fulfilled in His presence. He opens His heart to us and we begin to open our heart to Him.

Then as a result of this spiritual union between God and man we are given, in and through Him, the ability to spiritually conceive new life, in the same way, in principle, that a child is conceived in a marriage.

Heavenly:- From that day forward the seventh sense becomes active, and with faith and intent, the new born-again soul and spirit begins the journey of intimacy with God.

This state effectively begins to progressively allow the nature, character, love and power of God Himself to flow into and through our human faculties. This begins the process of redeeming and renewing our sixth sense, together with our body, soul, spirit, mind, will and emotions as well. Our conscience is enlivened to become fully aware of right and wrong, in any given situation, and our spirit, under the guidance of God, always causes us to want to do, and to actually do what is right!

The **fruits of the Spirit** can begin to flow into who we are and through us to others.

These are:-

love (unstoppable, inexhaustible heavenly affection),
joy (endless ability to experience a heavenly happiness, in the midst of the most difficult circumstances),
peace (an unending ability to stay calm and relaxed in every situation, and at one with God, self and man... even our enemies),
patience (never being anxious or impatient as we deal with life's trials),
kindness (able to show positive emotions, words and actions toward people when not feeling yourself, or even if they don't deserve it),
goodness (always wanting and doing the right thing),
faithfulness (hanging in there, even in the hardest of times and seeing things through to completion),
gentleness (softness and tenderness) and
self-control (able to contain and process negative emotions and turn them into positive).

We then find ourselves capable of operating in the **gifts of the Spirit.**

They are:-

word of wisdom (to know what to do in a given situation),
word of knowledge (God revealing secrets to you to help resolve issues),
faith (to believe for what ever God wants to do),
healing (able to declare healing of body, soul and

spirit, as and when the Lord instructs you to),
miracles (power to declare miracles according to the will and heart of God),
prophecy (speaking the words of God as instructed in any given circumstance),
discernment (knowing good from evil, right from wrong, truth from deception),
tongues (speaking in a heavenly language given uniquely to you), and
interpretation of tongues (able to understand the heavenly language that you or others have spoken).

In the process we are also able to operate and effectively use the **'full armour of God'**:-

helmet of salvation (our renewed mind protecting us from temptation),
breastplate of righteousness (our renewed heart showing us what is right and wrong),
sword of the Spirit (an intimate knowledge and commitment to the wisdom of the Bible, and being led day by day by the Holy Spirit of God),
shield of faith (belief that you truly are a child of God, a kingly priest and ambassador under the constant protection of God and the Host of Heaven),
belt of truth (our renewed spirit able to always tell the truth, deal honestly with people and with God, and able to discern the truth in others),
shoes of willingness to spread the gospel of peace (a passionate obedient heart spreading the love of The Lord Jesus and the Gospel of His cross), and
praying at all times in the Spirit (being in tune with His heart and power at all times, and always knowing how and what to pray).

Then we have all the fullest potential, to be all that we are destined to be, and do all that we are destined to do, in the power of God Himself, in the midst of what can be a hostile environment, until the earth is ultimately filled with the glory of the Lord, as the waters cover the sea, and the kingdoms of this world become the kingdoms of our God, and He will reign for ever and ever!

Chapter 10 - Advanced Attraction and Intimacy

I propose to go on now and describe at a much greater level of detail this mysterious love relationship between a man and women, and between each human being and God Himself.

To achieve the ideal pattern of this amazing love relationship here on earth, we need to apply the same principles, values, characteristics and boundaries that are meant to operate in the ideal heavenly model, into our earthly relationships here-and-now in the thrust and parry of daily life.

A young man for example usually at some stage in the normal course of his life will experience a natural inner desire and indeed compulsion to seek out an agreeable and compatible young woman of child bearing age, in order to build an enduring relationship together with her, with the ultimate expectation and outcome of an exclusive, dedicated, faithful, romantic and deeply intimate relationship with one another, including the wonderful privilege of mutual sexual intimacy, and seeking to ideally experience the wonder of the *gift of children*. I say gift because there is no guarantee of fruitfulness in this area. It is clearly a gift and blessing from God over which we have limited control and influence. Nevertheless, it is usually the dream of all young couples to ultimately have their own children and create a family unit. A young woman in the normal course of things will also experience this same desire and compulsion, often in different ways with differing emotions, intensity, goals, expectations and objectives, but these natural drives are however thoroughly complementary and consistent one with the other, and both have the same objective of going out into the big world to create what is ultimately known as a new family unit. Such new family units should ideally be based upon a strong network of loving, deeply held, committed, loyal, faithful and fulfilling covenant relationships. The relationship between a husband and a wife is the chief of these. It is the uniquely powerful, wonderful and intimate kernel of each new family unit.

A man or a woman, consciously or unconsciously, will ultimately seek out, or indeed long for, a loving life partner, but so too will they personally experience an inner drive, which is not always readily identified, to seek out and establish a unique personal and powerful connection with the One True and Living God! The combination of this couple-covenant-love for each other, together with their own individual and couple-love connections with God, have the potential to form the strongest most profoundly strategic and beneficial foundation, upon which to begin and continue a family's journey and destiny. It will set them in good stead here on earth and will ideally position all parties in preparedness for their eternal existence.

A man will also usually seek out a woman whom he finds attractive and desirable, open and honest, with emotional integrity and simplicity of heart. Who will honour him, respect him and love him, and who is genuinely keen to have children with him and make a family together. He will typically be attracted to a woman who will allow him and indeed encourage him to feel good about himself, and even if she feels she is more intelligent or better educated than he, will still make room for him to co-lead the marriage and the family, and have sufficient space and time to build confidence and to explore and grow as a man and a new husband and father. Often, he would like to solely provide for his new wife and family so that she doesn't have to work unless she wants to, but unfortunately that is not the norm these days, since both parties usually need to work in order to maintain a reasonable standard of living. Most men would also prefer not to be with a woman who is bossy, argumentative, negative, nagging, controlling, manipulative, stifling, jealous, critical, moody, vengeful, illogical or unreasonable, who refuses to quietly discuss issues and seek practical and pragmatic solutions together, both as a couple and as family.

A woman, on the other hand, will usually seek out a man whom she feels comfortable with, one who she finds handsome, attractive and desirable, and whom she believes also finds her attractive, lovable and desirable as well. She will typically seek out a man who will take care of her, and make her feel safe, loved, cherished, appreciated, honoured, protected and at-home... and whom she believes will find her truly adorable, as well as beautiful, cute and sexy, and with whom she will be highly valued and respected. She will also appreciate a man who allows her the freedom to dress and make herself feel pretty, both in her home and out in the community, and one whom is someone she can place her trust in at all times. Who will ultimately keep her safe and secure enough to settle down and have babies, if that is what her heart desires. A woman will also appreciate a man who is in touch with who he is, willing to talk about his feelings and opinions, confident in his capabilities and his masculinity, as well as thoughtful, understanding and respectful of the uniquely female aspects of his partner. She will value a man who is sensitive, caring and considerate especially in her times of feeling delicate, insecure and emotionally troubled. Finally, most women would prefer not to be with a man who is dominating, pushy, aggressive, argumentative, angry, violent, manipulative, overbearing, controlling, stifling, jealous, critical, moody, negative, or vengeful. Nor one who is addicted to any potentially anti-social vice, behaviour or substance including being engaged with pornography and sexual aberrations or modalities with which she is not comfortable. The wild and often intoxicating adventures of new romance will always ultimately have to settle down to the realities of a 'normal' life, whatever that may be, and it's always recommended to think about what that might look like before seriously starting out on the journey of love.

There are many very simple and practical things which a couple can do to help keep their marriage strong and well. Regular timeouts without the children for talking and sharing, date nights, going special places, having small inexpensive holidays, words of encouragement, helping each other with practical tasks, giving small gifts to each other, working on projects together, saving for future treats, plenty of time for casual and intimate touch and love making, and so on.

Relationship counselling or education has not been widely implemented in our community, but it is an extremely valuable, helpful and beneficial process to enter into before considering a serious, committed relationship. It allows a couple to explore all manner of important issues with an experienced counsellor, mentor or educator with a view to being better informed and prepared for serious relationship commitment. They typically consider issues like regular, open, honest, intentional communication, conflict negotiation, dealing with unspoken problems and issues, family of origin differences, choice of friends, existing friends, financial skills, management and practice, partner styles, relationship flexibility, relationship closeness, habits and character traits, leisure activities, sexual expectations, spiritual beliefs, parenting expectations, relationship satisfaction, assertiveness, self-confidence, avoidance, partner dominance, avoiding control mechanisms, dealing with stress, managing change, family organization, keeping the peace and so on. All of which are very practical and relevant to a good marriage. Each of which would be worthy of a book of their own, and many of which also apply to varying degrees in relationships with friends and family. I often use this as a check list to see how things are going in my own relationships and others with whom I work, please feel free to do the same.

Inner healing support, assistance and advice are also critical to minimizing difficulties which could be faced in a new covenant relationship. One cannot effectively have a strong healthy relationship with a spouse if we are hurting, broken, wounded or believing lies in our heart. It affects who we are and how we relate to each other. These processes usually address issues like, genuine belief in ourselves, believing that we are loved, that our sins are forgiven, that God loves us, and has our best interest at heart, avoiding harbouring offence, resolving past offences, lies that we believe, inner vows which are hurting us or others, saying we'll never do this or go there, or trust anyone again, and making snap judgments which are incorrect or unfair. Let's rather be believing the truth, that we are sons, friends, ambassadors and priests of God, allowing God to nurture us, as well as always loving others and allowing ourselves to be loved, dealing with hard hearts, dealing with curses which have been put on us or our family, walking in the light, having no secrets, being healed, and finding God's very best plan for our lives. These issues also apply equally to us singles.

As you can see, starting well, and sustaining a high-quality satisfying, fulfilling covenant relationship, requires a couple to consider a myriad of practical issues. Love is not all that you need! But *Real Love* together with the related very practical and do-able values, life skills and worldview, embodies all these issues and more, and gives us every chance of success in life. We need to be well prepared. I occasionally reflect again on my own situation, in that since becoming a single man again when my wife died, these types of issues are and would be of critical importance were I to consider remarriage. While we are never going to be perfect this side of heaven and neither will our potential partner, nevertheless, preparing well before committing or even allowing yourself to seriously consider falling in love, makes us better informed, reduces risk and makes us better equipped to deal with any challenges which may arise. Sometimes out of a fear of missing out on an opportunity we can make radical compromises in the hope of 'love making everything alright'. While this can often seem reasonable and logical, a really bad relationship can far outweigh any disadvantage of remaining single. I can see this clearly in my own situation. There is also a temptation to 'try before you buy' and just move in together as lovers and 'see how it goes'. This is not a viable alternative in that statistics thus far seem to indicate that generally greater than eighty percent of such relationships end in separation, and many are left with residual emotional pain and scars which tend to adversely affect our potential future relationships. Breaking up from such a relationship can have the same residual impact as divorce. Also, another serious community impact is that when this type of non-committed sexual relationship proliferates in a community the advent of serious sexually transmitted diseases quickly becomes endemic. Sadly, that is the situation today, in most of our societies.

So before committing to a sexually active romantic relationship it is worth some preparatory thought and reflection. Be very thoughtful about choice of partner. Are they a potential covenant marriage partner? If not, then why would one want to enter into what is in fact a de-facto marriage? As you can see commencing well and sustaining a high-quality satisfying and fulfilling covenant relationship, needs a couple to consider a myriad of practical issues. It's wise to think on these things before allowing ourselves to fall in love! Project our minds and hearts into the theoretical future, and reflect, is this the 'right' person? Is what is being proposed doable, viable or sensible? Is it even vaguely reasonable? And what would be the implications of such action? My experience is that when you step back and take some time out, relax, reflect and consult with God, you will find that the best course of action will start to become clear.

It's also important to consider another one of the eighty—twenty rules. In eighty percent of cases the couple will end up living where the wife comes from, where most of her key family members are living. My learning on this is that a woman, consciously or unconsciously, will feel better, safer and more supported amongst or closely located with her own family members, particularly while birthing and supporting young children.

Chapter 11 - Agape Based Marriage and Family

This chapter explores anecdotally, and at a high level, the ideal type of agape-love based marriage, family and friendships, based on my own experiences and learning, and those of colleagues and friends around me.

Agape love is that ideal love modelled and taught about by the Lord Jesus himself. It should optimally be present most, or all of the time, in marriage, family and related home life. The home is meant to be a peaceful, loving, affirming, safe place for every member of the family. Issues as they arise should be flagged by one or other of the family members, and should be taken seriously, and appropriate discussion and resolution entered into in the best interest of all concerned. For example, when Junie and I would have a disagreement, leaving the marriage or the family was not an option that was ever seriously considered! We took our vows very seriously and after sometimes experiencing initial frustration, disappointment, emotional pain or anxiety, usually caused by our inexperience at resolving such complications, we would cry, laugh, yell or jump up and down and let off steam, but then we would ultimately discuss, listen, clarify, understand, negotiate and come to some mutually agreeable solution. Then move on! Sometimes this would only take a few minutes, or hours. Very occasionally a whole day, or a few days, but that was not the norm and is not recommended, because it increases the pain levels and extends the emotional recovery period.

Our home was a place I loved to be. I had a wonderful, yet ridiculously intense, sixty hour a week senior management job for which I am ever grateful. Yet while I enjoyed the work immensely, the highlight of my day was to head home to my beautiful wife and family again. When my car mounted the crest of the hill near my home, and the vista of my beautiful, usually lush and green neighbourhood, spread out across the large undulating valley, up to the surrounding eucalypt forested hills... my heart skipped with joy and anticipation! Arriving home just a few short minutes later, I'd park the car, and then walking with a skip in my step, a sparkle in my eyes, and a deep longing and joy in my heart, to the front door of my home! There I would usually be met by the children first, bubbling excitedly with the news and adventures of the day, and then a big hug and kiss from my beautiful wife. This is something I still miss, in the deepest places of my heart and spirit, since she went home to glory! Then there were the inviting aromas of a home cooked meal lingering in the air. What magnificent and powerful loving experiences and memories these are. Though sadly, I rarely got home in time to eat with the children, I was usually able to see them and spend time with them before they went to sleep, and Junie would often hold back her own dinner so she could share the meal with me. These were sweet, delightful, satisfying and powerfully therapeutic life experiences. They bonded us together as a family and we had lots of fun and adventures together. These memories are myriad, and positive, gentle and deeply romantic to my heart, even today, some twenty years later. It is already seven full years since Junie died, and just last year I was driving home from a meeting in the city, my car mounted the crest of that all too familiar hill, and all of a sudden, those blissful memories of coming home to my treasured wife and family, flooded through my soul, melted my heart and filled me with a warm and delightful explosion of emotions! Then, as my favourite new car, which I brought in memory of Junie the year she died, began to descend that oh so familiar hill, my heart sank as I remembered she would not be there! She'd gone home to be with the Lord! This caused those familiar yearnings, longings and the deepest of tender loving emotions, to linger for a gentle winsome moment, then all too swiftly move on. Like the ghostly mist rising from cool landscape on the sunny morning of a promising new day. As always, I slowly lifted my spirit by inwardly celebrating and being thankful for that which I still had, rather than grieving for what had gone on before me. Marriage and family times are so precious, I cannot overstate them. It is worth every effort to seek to make our marriage and family really work and be an enjoyment for all concerned.

I remember times when we would go on holidays with the children sometimes to Queensland, our home state two thousand kilometres away. As the family got bigger, we bought family vans, Mitsubishi star wagons and such, so the kids had plenty of space and comfort in the car and we would drive, tag teaming two hours at a time, all the way to Queensland for a few weeks holiday and then drive all the way back. This was before all the latest social networking technology. We actually read books and told stories, listened to the radio playing music, sang songs and played crazy games. I spy! Are we there yet? Those were amazing bonding times of adventure, with our families and friends, which punctuated our otherwise very busy lives. One of Junie's favourite pastimes was to organize the details of our next family holiday, so we always had some rest and recreation to look forward to. She would work so very hard to see how many fun adventures we could fit into our sometimes very tight budget. Refreshing, encouraging, invigorating, and rejuvenating! We resolved that even when we could not really afford it we would still try to save and have a small holiday of some sort with our kids at least once a year.

There were tough times too. When we were first transferred to Melbourne from Queensland, Junie was seven months pregnant with our beautiful and gifted first daughter, who was born two months later into a new home we'd just moved into while I was still struggling to master a new and very challenging job. We were a couple who had only just been married barely two years, with absolutely no local family support! We were totally dependent on God alone! And these were tough times! Junie also experienced what we now call post-natal depression, which wasn't understood in those times. There were days when neither of us felt we would make it through the day! We were struggling and our new baby was struggling, but each day we asked for the help of God and each day we seemed to make it through! Some days Junie would say, "I just can't cope! I need you with me!" and most times I would be able to take a day off to be at her side, and to help with the baby. But then there were days when she would ask me, but I had committed to something really important at work where I would have let down and disrupted a large team of workmates, if I had not presented for work. So, with tears in our eyes and heavy hearts, we would hug longingly, and then part, and I would go to work, and by the grace of God and the faithfulness and strength of *Real Love*, passion and purpose I would come home, and all would be well! We had survived another day! Thank You Jesus! These were days when we learned to trust in God, and I saw the faithfulness of agape selfless love, demonstrated by my beautiful, young wife, as she battled to come to grips with motherhood for the first time, without the support of closely located family. These were tough times! But they built our character, and they strengthened our love and trust in God. Day by day, moment by moment, until at last we settled into our new neighbourhood, started attending church, met our neighbours and made new friends, and all too quickly our little one grew to be a healthy, clever, inquisitive, intuitive and adventurous young toddler who gave us so much joy. Two years later there was a little sister on the scene, and they became the best of friends, kindred spirits in life and mischief. She too was clever beyond her years, creative, intuitive, caring, determined, practical and purposeful. Children are such a delight and blessing and bring a lifetime of powerful learning places.

I also remember times where one of our family members would be sick or hurt. Some were really crazy accidents, some very serious illnesses, and the whole family would feel their pain, and experience varying degrees of disruption to our normal daily lives. But each time we would rally, work together, lay a plan, and do what needed to be done. Beyond that which was humanly possible, we would always cry out as a family to God in prayer! And ultimately, in His time He would bring healing and recovery!

We did projects together, had adventures together and enjoyed life to the full, with the limited time and meagre resources we had in those early days. As I look back, I don't regret a moment of my life! And it was the same with my precious Junie! As she was preparing to die, after just thirty-six wonderful years of marriage together! She lay there in her hospital bed, before she began to lose her faculties, through the agency of illness and medicine, looked into my eyes with the hint of tears, and with *Real Love*, passion, fulfillment and acceptance said, "Thank you for loving me! And all the amazing times we've shared together! I do not regret a moment! We have done everything I had ever dreamed of and so much more!" My eyes welled up with tears and we embraced longingly and wept together, probably for the last time really, as the days of palliative care commenced the very next day. It was soon after this momentous and eternally meaningful moment that Junie's little sister arrived all the way from Queensland within six hours of being informed of her beloved sister's impending death. This was a great encouragement to Junie, and to me, that she would come so quickly and without hesitation or delay. She was followed closely by all of her family except her little brother who we found out later was also in hospital struggling with a heart attack. Junie's family is a close unit of two brothers, four sisters and a mum, together with loads of precious aunties, uncles, cousins, nephews and nieces. Her dad had died years earlier. They all urgently sent representatives to Junie's side and they and my family was such a great encouragement to her and to me. Junie in her last few days/hours saw about forty different family and friends and greeted them, loved on them and blessed them with her last breaths. She was a good and faithful joyful loving woman, and my very best friend and lover, who demonstrated God's selfless love so well here on this earth. As do so many other faithful mums and single mums and the valiant men in their lives. Now as she walks in heaven along with Jesus, her heavenly bridegroom and hero! I celebrate her memory here on earth, and in this book! In these days, weeks, months and years of life, I learned the profound benefits, blessings and critical importance of marriage, family and friendships both on earth and in heaven!

Chapter 12 - Agape Based Church and Community

This chapter now seeks to deal with some discoveries, thoughts, observations and learning regarding the church of The Lord Jesus Christ. This unique and miraculous Divine entity, this wondrous and loving community, a peerless and in one sense ethereal spiritual ecclesia constitutes collectively the sole representative and witness of God Himself here on this earth. It is actually the combination of all people, young and old, over the face of the earth who have decided to *follow* Jesus, repented of doing things our own way and received personally, and by conscious and active decision, the loving act of redemption which He offers through His death and resurrection on the Cross. It is those of us who have asked Him to be Lord of our lives, and who are now actively engaged with Him, seeking to ensure that every person around the world gets the opportunity to know Him and has the freedom of choice to follow Him. People who are seriously seeking to apply Jesus' love, principles, values, and way of life... in their marriages, families, local churches, communities, cities, regions, states, nations... and internationally, in order that this world may in due course become the wonderful place that it is destined to be, governed by God Himself, in and through His people.

Every genuine Christian individual and community, in every Nation under the sun, form an indispensable and critically needed element of this mysterious *Body of Christ*, of which King Jesus is the undisputed head. The earthly separateness of these individual groups is of no consequence to God because He is eminently capable of seeing us all as one, and managing, overseeing and guiding us in ways that no human being could ever do. When we are all genuinely seeking and hearing from God about what it is we are meant to be doing, each in our own sphere of influence, we will begin to observe that there is an amazingly cohesive integrated plan being directed from heaven, to do what the church is destined to do - to spread His miraculous agape love (*Real Love*) across the whole earth. So that all will have the potential to hear of Him and the opportunity to know Him... and we will thereby be making disciples of all Nations. These earthly segments and entities which make up the church, have occurred and been created simply to make this global mission practically doable from an earthly perspective. It would not be humanly possible to physically organize all the followers of Jesus Christ in the whole world into a single integrated unit, like a large conglomerate. It was never His intention to do so. On current figures that would be significantly more than three or even four billion people by now! So, let's see each other as all members of the one big heavenly team led by God Himself and focus not on what is different, but upon the heart, seed and calling which we each carry, in order to bring in His Kingdom. If there are important issues or errors identified between us, it is through quality relationships, wisdom, humility, love and Divine guidance that we will be able to resolve any really important difference.

The *secret* of success of this *Body of Christ* is Divine *agape* love.

Let's look more closely at this wondrous love. It is Divine and it is heavenly... It is not earthly, finite, corrupted or constrained in nature. It is patient, kind, gentle, good, truthful, humble, caring, unselfish, peaceable, protective, magnanimous, benevolent, charitable, fatherly, motherly, brotherly, sisterly, trustworthy, trusting, hopeful, persevering, faithful, unfailing and eternal, always seeking the highest best good of the one being loved! It is impossible for humans in an unredeemed state to be able to fully give this type of love. Even in fact to receive it, because it is a life changing love, which alters hearts and people in a permanent and positive way just by its very presence and agency. It is the secret powerful element from heaven which makes it possible for us to live the Christian life. It is the essence of God himself which flows through our heart and spirit as we give ourselves to him in full surrender, and as we allow Him to heal us on the inside. We need to be healed on the inside in order not to inhibit or pollute its purity in any way, as it passes through us to others. It is the heavenly *voice*, the Divine *agent* which brings the good news of Jesus to those who haven't heard and sets us all free from darkness and depression. It is also the glue which binds us together even though we operate in different circles and in different ways, and the fruit, evidence and testimony which grows from our new-born hearts, the reflection of God's character seen through us, the heavenly agent which changes lives here on earth, the balm which heals the broken hearted and sets the captives free, bringing oil of joy to the mourning and garments of praise to those in despair. It is the grace which overlooks unimportant issues and focuses on that which is important, the heart of the matter, the higher agenda, the will of God Himself... which is ultimately all that matters... because He always knows what is best for the specific individual, the marriage, the family, the church, the community, city, region, state and Nation. He holds the ultimate big picture! His ideal heavenly plan! The best that we can do is fit in with God's plan. He always knows best and always has the best interest of every one of us on his heart!

This is what loving God ultimately and practically means. It is doing His heavenly will in each and every situation and all circumstances, because 'Daddy always knows best', and obedience is always better than rituals, promises and sacrifices. Loving God takes many other forms depending on your giftedness, calling and destiny. It can be praise and worship, intercession, prayer and dialog, learning at His feet, growing in grace and the knowledge of God, listening more carefully, speaking out His words, spending time with Him, giving, doing, strategizing together, doing assignments together, engaging in battle and mission together, seeking wisdom together, exploring faith, walking in hope, even playing and having fun together. There is no end to what loving God can mean practically and individually, but the ultimate act of loving God is to obey His commands, His commandments and His great commission! This is also the agape love, which is meant uniquely, especially and particularly in its purest form, to operate between brothers and sisters within each given element of the Body of Christ... and also whenever we meet or relate together across the body... from different individual branches or ministries of the church.

Then there is the 'loving of ourselves'. We have to look after ourselves in a practical, meaningful, comprehensive and multifaceted fashion, if we are to be able to love and help others effectively. To love ourselves we need to have our best interest at heart so that we are operating at our maximum potential in order to love and serve God. We need a balanced diet, fresh air, sunshine, basic exercise, time for celebration, fun, friends and community. We need to always be learning growing and developing in practical life areas and skills, ready and willing to attend to practical health issues. For example, toothache can kill you, as can sugar diabetes, heart conditions, infected toenails, malaria, flu, asthma, allergies etc. We need to be self-conscious enough to look after ourselves, with good advice and the guidance of God, so we are worthy and capable agents of the Kingdom of God. Having said that, even if we find ourselves having to deal with a critical disability or chronic illness that the Lord has not yet relieved us from, we can still make the best of where we are, serve God with our whole heart and be very effective and powerful in His Kingdom.

Furthermore, in order to be strong churches and communities we need to have strong, healthy marriages. We have touched on this before. Marriage should be the most fulfilling aspect of our earthly experience. I know it's easy to say and hard to do but it is worth the effort. I'm sure you've heard the expression 'happy wife, happy life.' Well, the reverse is also true, and when husband and wife are both truly happy this will revolutionize enjoyment of life. Notwithstanding the need to love ourselves as mentioned above, we should literally seek our partner's genuine happiness and life satisfaction as being equal to or higher than our own, second only to our relationship with God. Yes, it is complex. But it starts with selfless love (*Real Love*) for one another. The very first and best thing to do is increase the quality of couple communications. Take time to really listen to one another in an active and interested way. Concentrate on what each is saying, seek to fully understand, ask clarifying questions and take turns sharing, to the point where you both feel fully heard and understood. Then if there are still issues, you can work together on a mutually satisfying resolution. If there are issues with family or in-laws, talk about it, share pray and agree on a strategy together. Consider, 'What is my wife's highest best good? And what is my husband's? What do they need, dream of, what are their natural passions, hobbies, gifts, talents, careers, life interests? If they had more time and money, what would they love to do?' Attend to these things and seek God about what to do about them. Maybe you can both work together on some short-, medium- and long-term goals that you'd both really enjoy.

Relating to sex and love making. If we really love our partner, it is not good to insist on our own way at our own time, but rather ask your wife or husband what they really enjoy, what would increase their sexual pleasure and delight. Put them first! If both parties do this, it can improve lovemaking in marriage no end and increase overall marriage satisfaction beyond belief. Don't be afraid to be a little more creative and flexible in making love. There are many ways to enjoy one another sexually and these are worth exploring, within reason. Explore variety and mutual enjoyment and satisfaction together, different times, places, positions and methods. It is not advisable however to explore that which seems to be an aberration, or indeed something which is not exclusive to the marriage couple alone, to normal natural male - female intimacy, or anything which one party feels is demeaning, embarrassing, shameful or they just simply do not enjoy. It is also counter-productive to withhold lovemaking from one another due to disagreement or as a perceived emotional punishment. It is usually possible to meet each other's important sexual needs, even if not totally in the mood or able to fully respond. These issues are also really important to marriage satisfaction and enjoyment.

Loving each other within the family is also really important. Some keys I have discovered are: Always put God first in everything and ideally always hold your marriage relationship as more important in the hierarchy of family relationships. That is, the needs of the husband and wife are important and often need to be satisfied or resolved before one can fully and effectively resolve challenges with the children. Try not to disagree on the way you deal with the children. If you have differences, try to resolve them with each other and be prepared to compromise. Because one or the other often sees things differently and this difference can add perspective which always needs to be seriously considered. Also, as the children get older it is often appropriate to include them in some of the discussions, when you are trying to make a call on a decision relating to them personally. Try to make sure the children always feel loved even if they have to be punished or grounded for something. Never withdraw your Agape love. *Real Love* is never withdrawn from the object of love but there always need to be boundaries to love. The children may want something that the family just cannot reasonably afford, it is not good to go into unreasonable debt to fulfil a family member's wants. However, sometimes there are needs which the family can work toward supplying creatively together. Some children may try to play mum and dad off against each other by seeking to cut a deal separately with the most agreeable partner. It's okay for one partner to assist in family negotiations on behalf of a child, but not for the child to seek to take advantage or be dishonest in their dealings. Family rules need to be Jesus based and fair, just, reasonable, doable and sometimes open to a little flexibility and trust... within reason, and somehow, we each have to build trust between one another within the family, even when we know that the said person is going to have difficulty fulfilling the agreement. For example, in the case of a young lady wanting to go out with new older boyfriend! Very tricky! Its best to try to agree on principles and methods before it happens rather than embarrassingly trying to resolve things under pressure in the heat of a real situation. A teenager, boy or girl, maybe bullying one or other of the parents. This is not on! A really difficult situation is where one parent has made an edict or punishment or such, during the day, which the other spouse when they come home and hear the circumstances from all parties, actually disagrees with the ruling! Very challenging! However, if one applies *Real Love*, honour, respect, openness, prayer and always wanting to achieve the highest best outcome for everyone, usually the matter can be resolved. But one has to be true to oneself, fair and reasonable, and able to justify what is done and said to all parties, which hopefully will achieve mutual consensus. However, sometimes compromises do need to be made. We could share on these issues for ages, but I think this will suffice.

There is also a Jesus expectation to love each other, in a community and as neighbours. This is a little more challenging because one cannot assume that the other party agrees with the Christian based principles that you may choose to apply in life and relationships. However, because of the generally positive, logical and reasonable nature of Judeo-Christian values and principles, most people will accept rulings made within those parameters. I try to apply the same Christian principles in every domain of life, in order to reduce stress and conflict and having to keep track of differences. Therefore reiterating, the overarching principles of love... are desiring the highest best for the other person and seeking to honour and obey God in all things, and these apply ideally in all cases. For example, I often find myself having to attend or chair meetings in all types of situations. I just generally apply basic governance principles to operate the meeting but then seek to apply Godly principles over and above those in order to generally create a positive, constructive, open, honest atmosphere, sticking to truth etc. This works very well generally. Sometimes for example one member at the meeting may be sounding off and getting angry and aggressive about a perceived injustice, wrong opinion or incompetence. Instead of shutting them down I give them a few minutes, and seek to hear what they are really saying, and why... and what the issues really are... endeavouring at all times to help resolve these basic issues, and give some immediate and hopefully helpful, honest feedback. If necessary, offering to follow the matter up outside of the meeting. There can sometimes be political machinations, potential coups, or 'silly-beggar' behaviour going on in a public meeting. So, I then seek to bring it out in the open, either privately, and/or in public, so the matter can be aired for what it is, and hopefully resolved, in an agreeable and helpful way, that is in the best interest of the group, as well as the larger organization or entity of which it is a part. Every group in our society is technically and potentially a part of something bigger than itself, and in some way or another directly or indirectly will affect the best interest of the city, region, Nation etc. Every situation is therefore always within the overarching parameters of what would God want, what is in the best interest of all concerned, and where does it fit in His big plan.

Agape love is not meant to be a wimpy, compliant, politically correct, wishy-washy love either. Applying love in a community situation may mean standing up and taking strong leadership on matters of principle, values, integrity and best interest of community and such, or standing against something which is inappropriate, or for something which is really important... and being prepared, confident, articulate and rational as to why this is so. Sometimes you may meet smiling assassins in life which I have described at some length in my second book and articulated an effective strategy to deal with such people. The overall, loving outcome will be to have community groups where everyone feels welcome, even if they have contrary opinions, everyone feels heard, honest questions are always answered, robust discussion is allowed, everyone is reasonable and logical, open to considering different ideas and issues, only the truth is spoken with love and respect, and where possible, the most optimal actions are always taken, which are mutually agreed and supported as being in the best interest of all. This is sometimes difficult, but it is achievable, and I have presided over many such situations, which have started out in difficulty, and ended up with overall congeniality and mutually agreed positive outcomes and relationships.

Finally, I'd like to briefly explore some of the differences between how agape love should generally operate between marriage partners as opposed to generally in a church or community at large. Firstly, the practical and emotional issues, goals and principles like active, positive and thoughtful communication and conflict resolution should always apply in every situation! The major difference however is that within a marriage, agape love should be applied together with intimate, open, honest, deep, vulnerable, passionate, mutually enjoyable, delightful and respectful sexual lovemaking. Whereas outside of a covenant marriage relationship, contrary to the opinions of some liberal folk, the act of making love, sexual intercourse and deep physical intimacy should not apply. This is in the best interest of all of society including the wellbeing of the Nation. It is not just some prudish religious stance to spoil our fun, but rather a pragmatic response to a myriad of seriously negative social, political, emotional, physical, economic and psychological consequences of such behaviours. And yes, this abstinence from sexual relationships outside of a covenant marriage relationship is of course, clearly articulated in principle as being one of the ideal model relationship instructions from God Himself.

In the same way that being unfaithful to the one true and living God by innocently or arrogantly, worshipping, serving and loving other gods, actually dishonours both God himself and the worshipper...

And because of the fact that He has given earthly marriage as a model example of the type of love relationship we are supposed to have with Him... So too does He expect us, to be intensely and intimately faithful to our marriage partners!

Looking back now it was mysteriously fortuitous, that at the same time I was 'prompted' to seek out a serious life partner, so too was I intentionally 'directed' on this convoluted journey all over Queensland, which ultimately and specifically 'brought' me to the very place where I would discover my wonderful wife, June. I had come from a very tiny country town just two hundred kilometres away, and after traveling all over the country on relieving staff, where I could have just as likely met my future wife, I had now arrived at the larger provincial town of Kingaroy, where I stayed for such a short while. There I had met friends of friends, of whom I enquired, and ultimately went to that place of destiny. Where I was immediately 'drawn' towards this young woman in particular, across a large room crowded with all manner of other beautiful women, yet 'strangely' I felt deeply *attracted* to just this *one* simple, elegant, adorable, country beauty!

I should mention at this point, that this type of heavenly purpose and intentionality has been with me since the day I was born. I have known the unseen presence of a loving and personal God on the journey of life, I have sensed his hand of protection upon me and my family and been strongly aware of His guidance. He has led me from one Divine appointment to another... and one learning place to another. I sensed destiny when I was baptized at six years of age, was drawn by His personal call at twelve years of age, and at sixteen I 'fell in love' with Him and His great cause of the Kingdom of God!... And even though I did not imagine the ways that He would lead me and use me, I always felt a call of destiny in my heart! Such are the plans and purposes of our omnipotent and loving God. Some say these are all coincidence and random events, but I have journeyed with Him long enough to know that it was, that it is... Destiny! And just as I systematically courted Junie and sought to win her heart, so too does our loving God exhaustively, tirelessly and continually court us and seek to win our hearts! He is in fact courting every man woman and child on the face of this earth to give every one of us the opportunity to join him in eternal love and friendship. All we have to do is be listening intently, and be aware, ready to respond to His call. Junie was ready! Her heart was open. Another young man had already wounded her precious, delicate heart, but she had the courage to try again, as she was seeking intently with all of her heart to find her destiny lover. So too should we be seeking to find God our creator. He is so gentle yet persistent with each one of us... nurturing, wooing, attracting, seeking and calling. There is no end to His love and patience toward all of us. Some of us don't feel that we are worthy of His call. Like Cinderella might have felt, with her Prince Charming! But I want to assure you of His great love, and if you ask Him, He will assure you personally too. A still small voice, a strong thought, a deep feeling, something tangible in your body, He is unlimited in His ability to connect, and surprise! But please don't be afraid to ask, to reach out to Him! Read His book, listen to His music and consult with His followers! He intensely desires us to become aware of His presence, so that we may share together with Him, and learn what we need to know in order to enjoy life's journey and be prepared for eternity. Every time I have asked The Lord a serious question on which I was prepared to take decisive action in my life and circumstances, He has always answered me. The Holy Book says that if we seek Him with all our heart... He will be found by us!

Having fully engaged in relationship with God it is then intended that He and His devotees should enjoy a close and intimate one to one relationship, in the same manner that a married couple should do. It does not mean that humans are intended to have physical sex with God, although sadly this is the way that demonic powers can sometimes seek to emulate or counterfeit the wonderful emotionally, spiritually and intellectually intimate and satisfying relationship ... that Judeo- Christian disciples are meant to have with God. Some people even try to fill this conscious or unconscious void in their life, through lack of connection with God, by trying to emulate that deeply felt insightful and orgasmic-like experience which they are longing for, through the use of what are often illicit and illegal hallucinatory substances.

A genuine and fully developed relationship with God is meant to be close, committed, dedicated, passionate, faithful, open, honest, trusting, no-secrets, intimate, loving, vulnerable, euphoric, and entered into the exclusion of all other 'gods'. Such 'other-gods' can typically be anything that we have allowed to come between us and God, or to be a distraction or diversion. Thus, causing us consciously or unconsciously, wilfully or naively to allow ourselves to be drawn away from God, towards infidelity. You may indeed question whether our relationship with God is meant to be personal, close, intimate and even euphoric. However, my experience is that whenever I have an encounter with God, no matter how distant He may have felt or how fleeting the moment may have seemed, it is always deeply meaningful, healing, soothing, helpful, emotional, enlightening, up-lifting, satisfying, unique and moving... and more and more these days, actually physically tangible and detectable by our five human senses. I believe this is a manifestation of the statement that in the last days He will pour His Spirit out on all flesh.

From time to time, usually when I have been most in need, I have seen glimpses of vistas in heaven which have given me goose bumps and taken my breath away. For example, God sitting on His throne in heaven and overseeing what is going on locally and around the Universe. Recently I saw Him riding a magnificent beautiful white battle horse. Quite often when I come to a new country or location... or when I stand to speak, teach, preach or minister, or all of the above... the Lord will give me a vision for the people in the place where I find myself... and as I have shared these over the years and heard how they were typically powerful, accurate, helpful, healing, strategic and directional... I have been particularly encouraged to continue to include this type of ministry, as the Lord enables, on each occasion I have the privilege to minister. I have also heard small single phrases and sentences from The Lord which have changed my life for ever and led to massive new directions and experiences in life. Some examples have been... "You will go to the Nations!"... "Your son will be born in

January when you were!" Which he was!... and "If your wife dies, I will raise up 10,000 other passionate people behind her and they will see millions come in to the Kingdom of God!" Which they are... and "You are my beloved son in whom I am well pleased and when the wound in your heart is healed, you will be capable of love beyond your wildest imagination!" Which I am experiencing in an increasing capacity and liberality every day! I often sense a love so strong that wells up within me when I see situations and people which need loving attention, support or encouragement ... and when praying for people, a flood of love overflows my heart... words of encouragement, declaration, prophecy, wisdom and healing come to mind, and I find my hands burn with the intensity of what The Lord is doing in that moment. This is not something unique to me but is available in one form or another, at the loving infinitely wise will and discretion of God, to any and all followers of the Lord Jesus Christ.

One of my most recent experiences of this type was that I was standing in my bedroom one morning feeling quite sad and sorry for myself as I occasionally do since my wife died. I felt tired, weary, lonely, sorrowful, troubled, low in spirit, energy and morale... when all of a sudden, I sensed someone was standing behind me and felt what seemed to be two strong, gentle, warm and loving hands on my shoulders. I glanced in the mirror to see who was there, but He was completely invisible to my normal eyes. Immediately my body, soul and spirit were flooded with the most amazing combination of feelings as I sensed something awesome flow through His hands into my body. I call it unction for want of a better word. It was warm, comforting, encouraging and peaceful... my energy levels lifted, my head cleared, emotions swung to the positive and sorrow turned to joy in an instant. Then His voice (because I realized after a few seconds that I was in the presence of the Lord Jesus Christ) spoke softly, but with firm intent and He said "Get ready! Its already started!" I immediately knew that he was referring to the great Spiritual Awakening which I was already concluding, from my visits and friends all over the world, was well under way. This word was a strong confirmation to my heart and has served to always focus and energize me personally on that which is of the greatest importance... the advancement of the Kingdom of the Lord Jesus Christ, in every Nation all over the earth! The Church of The Lord Jesus Christ is both the agent and outcome of this great Awakening... and agape Love (*Real Love*) is the essence and power of the campaign. It is said that all will know that we are followers of the Lord Jesus Christ because of the way we *Love One Another*.

There is one other manifestation of *Real Love* which is extra critical in our time and that is the love of the Nation and people of Israel. In this age in which we are living there are dark spiritual forces in the earth seeking to dominate our societies and destroy our way of life... and one outworking of this is an unreasonable and inexplicable hatred and destructive attitude toward Israel and the Jewish people. There is often a deadly attitude in some places towards followers of the Lord Jesus Christ as well, but the intensity of this hatred and ill will is particularly strong toward Israel. Followers of the Judeo- Christian way must stand with our brothers the Jews, in these most difficult and uncertain times... with vehement and faithful friendship and solidarity... and in the unending and inexhaustible life-giving flow and power of agape love. Masada must never fall again! And His people will remain in *their* own Land... until He Comes!

Chapter 13 - Agape with Enemies

Followers of Jesus also have values and instructions that exhort us to love our enemies and deal lovingly with all people, even though they may not deserve it. This love is demonstrated in the selfless way that Jesus died and rose again, so that the sins of all human-kind may potentially be forgiven. He is our model in that He died for us, though we were still sinners and enemies of goodness... and we did not deserve Him doing so. Thus, we are expected to extend the same love and privilege that He gave to us, to all people on the face of the earth, even those who are or would like to be considered our enemies. The secret is this: Agape love as already stated is the most powerful agent for life change that exists in the whole universe. There is no person and no situation that cannot eventually be changed by the power of love. Every Nation and every people-group acknowledge the importance of love and exemplify it in their culture for example through the honour, respect and importance paid to romance, marriage, family, community and such. Even though some cultures do not strongly emphasize agape love, every people group has the potential to be conquered by love. Even the most evil, corrupt and cruel of people can be impacted and ultimately changed by the power of love. Evil tries every trick to stop this love coming to influence. Some cultures try to stop their people hearing about the Gospel of the Lord Jesus Christ, but this will not be effective. The Word is out! The Good News about Jesus is breaking out across all barriers and borders and the Tidal Wave of Love is building up in volume and intensity and will ultimately become unstoppable. The hearts of hurting, lonely, stressed, enslaved, abused, abandoned, brain washed people are all beginning to hear about Jesus Love! The message is going out by all means, everywhere.

Agape also works effectively in even the most hostile of environments. If your enemy hurts you, you are meant to respond to him in love. If he curses you, you bless him, asking God to deliver him from the darkness in which he finds himself. Ask the Lord Jesus to visit him in his dreams and speak to him of eternal life. When your enemy is influenced, controlled, manipulated by demons, spirits and gins, ask the Lord to bind these powers of evil and send them to the pit of hell where they belong. Ask Him to set the people free of any curses or bondages, even if they have purposely brought the situation upon themselves! This then allows the individuals to discern more clearly... so they can see things as they really are, discern truth from lies, overcome the power of brainwashing, and receive healing of their spirits! Where they are in darkness bring them into the light. If in bondage set them free. Change the hearts of evil leaders or remove them from power. Let the 'grass roots' rise up and cry out for truth and freedom, which can only come from the Lord Jesus Christ. Let love, joy, peace, patience, kindness, goodness, faithfulness, gentleness and self-control be their practical reality. Let occult practices and crafts of demons and evil spirits, of curses and spells and such, cease in the Powerful Name of Jesus! This is the wonder of His Miraculous Agape Love.

When someone attacks you, don't take it personally. Our true enemies are not flesh and blood people but rather the demons which seek to goad people directly or indirectly to do evil. Say for example, "I love you but I will not allow you to treat me in this way". "I release you from that which goads you to do evil in Jesus Powerful Name!", "No matter what you do I will never stop loving you!", "I want to see you free from this nonsense and atrocity which you are currently perpetrating!" Does this mean that agape love always requires the individual to be 'nice' to everybody? Not at all! While grace, gentleness, love and kindness are the starting point and preferred approach, sometimes one will face an enemy so hard-core evil and unrepentant, that the only effective approach will be to take up arms against him and bring him down. The ideal way to do this is through righteous, just and loving police forces, security agencies and defence forces... in lieu of disorganized or indeed organized rebellion, anarchy or civil war. This action has been necessary a number of times this last century in order to deal with those who would seek to set up cruel, dark, undesirable, authoritarian administrations and governments. Hitler was a classic example. We need to continue to strongly oppose and resist such activities by ruthless and dark dictators, individuals and organizations who would force people to comply with their philosophy... and punish people by death if they choose to believe or do otherwise.

When individuals, communities and Nations choose to live by agape love there is no need for draconian laws and control mechanisms. These people naturally do what is good and right, fair, just and free. In situations where this type of evil is able to rise up to bring opposition to Godly law and order, it means that the Nation has not allowed and encouraged the Gospel of the Love of The Lord Jesus Christ to spread and grow freely within the land. This is counterproductive to all concerned. That's why there always needs to be freedom of religion and thought, and everyone must have a chance to hear His Gospel and have an opportunity to follow Him and adopt His way of life. This is the only answer to the world's problems. Real and positive change needs to occur in the hearts of individuals, and this will ultimately change Nations into the idyllic societies which we are meant to be, which we are exhorted to be, and which the Lord has modelled for us in various ways throughout the generations.

Chapter 14 - Miracles and Mysteries of Agape

I am sure you know personally or have heard of many testimonies where acts of selfless love have caused miracles to occur and lives and societies to be changed. Jesus' death and resurrection is the prime model example which has changed the world for ever and for the better. We need to stop trying to reduce the foundational and day-to-day influence that the Judeo-Christian way has upon our Nations. This way of life is so sweet and beneficial to our societies that reducing it dilutes, pollutes and even degrades our way of life. If allowed to continue, its absence would actually lead to destruction of many of the positive values and freedoms which we hold so dear, yet have often taken for granted. Situations which come to mind for me where the Judeo- Christian way has directly or indirectly brought profound and positive influence on our society and way of life are:-

- Teaching us to love God, love others, love enemies, love and care for ourselves
- Spreading the message and example of this Jesus-love across the whole earth
- Encouraging all Nations and all peoples to love Him and live in and by His Love
- Saturating every element of our societies with the love of Jesus
- Emphasizing peace, cooperation and industry rather than warring and fighting
- Introducing democracy rather than rule by despots, tyrants, dictators and warlords
- Separation of powers and introducing

accountability and 'doing the right thing'
- Emphasizing truth, integrity and high ethical standards in society and life
- Encouraging societies to value the lives and worth of all individuals
- Introducing the concepts of rights, freedoms, privileges and responsibilities
- Introduction of equality for all men, women and children
- Sharing of resources and providing for people in need in our communities
- Seeking to stop trafficking and abuse of human beings
- Seeking to minimize or indeed stop self-destructive behaviours like drug usage
- Elimination of slavery and all forms of human forced work or degradation

These characteristics and values all emerge naturally, and by instruction, from the Judeo-Christian way of life.

Chapter 15 – Conclusion

In summary, *Real Love* is that love which is called *agape*... the heavenly love modelled by the Lord Jesus Christ and defined and recorded in His Holy Bible. This is the type of love that Judeo-Christian disciples of The Lord seek with His help, guidance, enabling and empowering, to live out in a practical way in their daily lives. This way of life and model example has been with us from the very beginning and has been increasing in visibility, clarity, pervasiveness and influence over the course of history as God has nurtured us on this 'love-journey' toward heaven and eternity. It can rightly be said that this life here on earth is a training ground for eternity. What we do here affects the world in which we live, echoes in eternity and ultimately has a direct impact on our eternal destiny. Some have sought to infer that Judeo-Christianity is a relatively young way of life, in order to advance the cause of other philosophies, however its foundations were clearly embodied in the creation event and in every phase and moment of history since. The Holy Bible unfolds this evidence progressively throughout its pages. It is well worth a read! But I suggest you start with the New Testament and then go back to read the Old. It is also powerful and beneficial as you read to ask God to help you understand the words and progressively unfold the mystery of His love story to you. You will be astounded at what wisdom and enlightenment is embodied in this miraculous book, and how it begins to emerge and make sense to you.

You will also find that all ways of life which have some beneficial truths within them, including those which some refer to as 'religions', have drawn these positive elements directly or indirectly from the Judeo-Christian Way. The Way of Agape Love! That which comes directly from the Heart of God!

You may also encounter the idea that there are many ways to God... and while this is a half-truth in that many can and have found the One True and Living God by approaching Him from a myriad of different directions, circumstances and life journeys... There is however only one true God... and only one way been made available to have access to and relationship with Him. That is by way of the Cross of The Lord Jesus Christ! His redemptive death, resurrection and the cleansing life-changing power of His blood... which was shed for us on Calvary's hill!... and this is required to be activated personally by way of conscious choice and response... from each and every individual who is desiring to enter into this God-relationship. There are no exceptions! Yet neither is anyone excluded! All people have been called, and are continually being called, to join Him in this covenant love relationship. He is the Bridegroom, and individually and collectively, we are the Bride! His heart and His intentions are toward us. His longing, yearning, deep, passionate, powerful, life changing love is crying out to us across time and history. All that is required is for us to respond... and then to go on and live a life of peace, joy, hope, love and freedom, as well as commitment and sacrifice. Then as we grow as individuals to be more like Jesus, we will apply ourselves toward the needs of others who have not yet heard His Voice or are indeed struggling to respond.

The effective wide-spread appropriation and application of this Love is truly the ultimate *Secret of Achieving a Wonderful World!*

In conclusion, I wish to Thank You deeply and sincerely for taking the time to come with me on this journey... and I trust it has been of some benefit to you, as it has been for me, as I have attempted to faithfully record this account of my own *Real-Love* story!... And whether you are married, have ever been married, or are single like I am now... there is a place for all of us, and opportunity for a heavenly marriage to the Lord Jesus Christ, the eternal Bridegroom! He is available to us right now, irrespective of whether we ever experience a true and loving marriage here on this earth. Furthermore, there is also an amazing earthly family...the Family of God, which is open now for all of us to be a part... in which we can enjoy the most delightful and fulfilling *Real Love* relationships all the days of our earthly lives!

And finally, I pray God's very best blessings upon you and yours, and that His Presence, Favour, Guidance, Wisdom and Love will always be with you as you journey daily on your own *Real-Love* adventure!

THE END

www.ingramcontent.com/pod-product-compliance
Lightning Source LLC
Chambersburg PA
CBHW050316010526
44107CB00055B/2270